ECCE AENEAS

Selections from Virgil's *Aeneid*
Books I and II

An edition for schools prepared by
HENRY L PHILIP

as a follow-up reader to
ECCE ROMANI

by permission of the
SCOTTISH CLASSICS GROUP

OLIVER & BOYD

Acknowledgments
We are grateful to the following for supplying photographs and giving permission for their use: The Mansell Collection, pp. 17, 59, 61; Ronald Sheridan's Photo-Library, pp. 39, 43. The illustrations on the cover and p. 40 are reproduced by Courtesy of the Trustees, The National Gallery, London.

Illustrated by Michael Strand and John Marshall

Oliver & Boyd
Robert Stevenson House
1–3 Baxter's Place
Leith Walk
Edinburgh EH1 3BB

A Division of Longman Group UK Ltd

First published 1986

ISBN 0 05 003839 7

Set in Linotron Times Roman 11 on 12pt and 11 on 14pt

Produced by Longman Group (F.E.) Ltd
Printed in Hong Kong

·CONTENTS·

Notes on cross-references

(a) AIC refers to the section headed Arrival in Carthage.
     LDOT refers to the section headed The Last Days of Troy.

Where line references appear without the prefix AIC or LDOT,
they refer to lines within the same main section as the note.

(b) References to the Language Notes (pp. 110–120) are prefixed
     LN #.

·TO THE TEACHER·

With ever-increasing pressures on the timetable, not only has the time available for the teaching of Latin in schools been greatly curtailed, but it is also becoming common for pupils to start Latin much later than they used to. These pressures, combined with the fact that the study of Latin is no longer limited to the top streams in selective schools, have forced Classics teachers to carry out a critical review of their schemes of work. There is a danger that, in this revision, certain authors, particularly the poets, will be omitted completely on the grounds that they are too difficult.

One poet who must clearly be at risk is Virgil since it is generally thought that he is much more difficult than, say, Ovid. But is he? As must be obvious to anyone who has searched for suitable passages for unseen translation, the trouble with Virgil is, not that he is difficult, but that in the midst of relatively easy passages there inevitably appear sections which are very difficult indeed.

The present book has been put together on the principle that edited versions of prose authors have successfully dealt with the problem of restricted time. Why should the same not happen for poetry?

By concentrating mainly on the narrative and removing some of the more bewildering passages such as Aeneas' encounters with Venus, I have tried to produce a school text which could be tackled by pupils aiming at either SCE Standard Grade or GCSE. Although my main concern has been to help pupils to read the text quickly, with understanding and, I hope, with some enjoyment, attention has also been paid to such matters as background, word order, rhythm, sound and figures of speech where it is felt that these will produce a greater appreciation of the poetry.

In the same way, without becoming involved in grammatical and textual niceties which will become part of the syllabus for those who wish to pursue the subject in more depth at a later stage, an attempt has been made to build up some knowledge of the main aspects of Virgil's grammatical usage. The book could be tackled at three different levels of study:

(a) a very swift translation, skimming over the most difficult Latin by using the glosses provided;

(b) a careful study of the literal translation to see how the idiomatic translation was arrived at; and

(c) an in-depth study, involving figures of speech and a study of the Language Notes.

It is for the teacher to decide which approach suits his/her pupils best.

·THE STORY OF THE AENEID·

Publius Vergilius Maro was born in 70 BC and died in 19 BC. His patron was Octavian who later became the Emperor Augustus. It was to glorify the achievements of Augustus that he wrote the epic poem called the *Aeneid* which describes the noble origins of Rome.

According to legend, Rome was founded by Romulus, a direct descendant of Iulus who landed in Italy with his father, Aeneas, after their escape from Troy; and since Aeneas was the son of Anchises and the goddess Venus, the founder of Rome himself can thus be said to be of divine descent. It was also claimed that the Julian **gens**, to which Augustus belonged, was descended from Iulus, so that Augustus too was ultimately of divine descent.

The *Aeneid* is a very long poem. The sections which are contained in this book describe how Aeneas and his followers were driven by a storm on to the shores of Carthage where he was welcomed by Queen Dido, herself a fugitive from the Phoenician city of Sidon, and how he related to her the story of the fall of Troy at the hands of the Greeks.

The remainder of the *Aeneid* tells of the many hardships and challenges which Aeneas had to face, including the loss of his father, being forced by the gods to suppress his love for Dido, a visit to the underworld to see for himself the future glories of Rome, and facing the hostility of the Italian tribes before he could fulfil his destiny and finally settle in Latium.

tantae molis erat Romanam condere gentem.

·THE VERSE USED BY VIRGIL·

1 *Quantity*

In English verse, we scan the lines by stressing certain syllables:

e.g. *Máry hád a líttle lámb.*

Latin verse depends on a different principle, that syllables are either 'heavy/long' (marked –) or 'light/short' (marked ᴜ), depending on the length of the syllable. 'Long' means the length of time the vowel is held, like a musical crotchet (♩) or quaver (♪).

(a) Some syllables are long because the vowel in the syllable is naturally long:

e.g. **canō, quī, prīmīs, ōrīs, vēnit, fātō.**

(b) Some syllables in which the vowel is pronounced as short are nevertheless scanned as long because the whole syllable takes longer to say. This happens where the vowel is followed by two consonants, whether these consonants are in the same word or not ('long by position'):

e.g. **nĕc** but **nēcdum, fuĭt** but **fuīt Tyrii, ĭn** but **īn latus.**

However, if the second consonant is **l** or **r**, the poet may treat the syllable as long or short as he pleases:

e.g. **pătrem** or **pātrem.**

No notice is taken of the letter **h**, which is not regarded as a consonant, or of the letter **u** in a **qu** combination.

(c) Diphthongs, i.e. two vowels which are sounded as one (**ae, oe, au, eu, ei, ui**), are long:

e.g. **Troiāē, prōēlium, claūstrum, Ēurus, dēīnde, cūī.**

(d) Otherwise, when two vowels come together, the first is almost always short:

e.g. **Italĭam, tenŭere, interĕa.**

(e) A vowel, diphthong or syllable ending in **-m** is elided if it comes at the end of a word and is immediately followed by a word beginning with a vowel or an **h**, i.e. for the purposes of scansion it is treated as if it were not there:

e.g. **lītŏrǎ; mūlt(um) īll(e) ēt tērrīs iāctātŭs ĕt āltō**.

(f) When it appears before a vowel, the letter **i** is sometimes a consonant (sounded like the English letter **y** as in 'yes'), sometimes a vowel:

e.g. **pāriĕtĭbus** (four syllables)   **Ĭūlŭs** (three syllables)
     Iūnōnĭs (three syllables)   **Ĭōpās** (three syllables)
     dīsiēctǎm (three syllables)

2 Dactylic Hexameter

There were many verse patterns in Latin poetry. The one which Virgil uses in the *Aeneid* is the Dactylic Hexameter. This line has six feet, which are like bars of music, and each foot is
     either a *Dactyl*   (long short short – ∪ ∪)
     or a *Spondee* (long long – –)
In a Hexameter, the fifth foot is almost always a Dactyl, and the sixth foot is always a Spondee or a Trochee (–∪).

The first four feet can be any mixture of Dactyls or Spondees. The normal pattern for the Hexameter therefore is:

$$\left.\begin{array}{c} - \ - \\ - \ \cup\cup \end{array}\right| \left.\begin{array}{c} - \ - \\ - \ \cup\cup \end{array}\right| \left.\begin{array}{c} - \ - \\ - \ \cup\cup \end{array}\right| \left.\begin{array}{c} - \ - \\ - \ \cup\cup \end{array}\right| \left.\begin{array}{c} \\ - \ \cup\cup \end{array}\right| \left.\begin{array}{c} - \ - \\ - \ \cup \end{array}\right.$$

By varying the pattern, the poet can produce different sound effects and moods:

e.g. speed and excitement in

    īnsĕquĭ|tūr clā|mōrquĕ vĭ|rūm strī|dōrquĕ rŭ|dēntŭm

toil and struggle in

    ērrā|bānt āc|tī fā|tīs mǎrĭ|(a) ōmnĭǎ| cīrcŭm

3 The Caesura //

Because the line is so long, there is usually a breathing pause, called a caesura, between words in either the third or the fourth foot:

e.g. ārmă vǐ|rūmquě că|nō,//Trō|iāe quī| prīmŭs ăb| ōrīs
or Itălĭ|ăm, fā|tō prŏfŭ|gūs//Lā|vīnăquě| vēnĭt

A caesura can appear in other feet, however, usually to produce some dramatic effect. For example, there is a very strong break in the second foot in

hāstām

cōntōr|sīt.// stĕtĭt|īllă trĕ|mēns,// ŭtĕ|rōquě rĕ|cūssō
(LDOT 38–9)

Compare
īntēn|dūnt.// scān|dīt fā|tālīs| māchĭnă| mūrōs
fēt(a) ār|mīs.//
(LDOT 125–6)
See also LDOT 131, 224, 228, 307, 341, 346, 366, 491.

4 Rhythmic Reading

To begin with, until you have learned the verse rhythm, you may find it helpful to stress the first syllable of each foot as in the following English line:

'Dówn ĭn ă / deép dárk / déll săt ăn / óldców / múnchĭă ă /
beánstálk.'

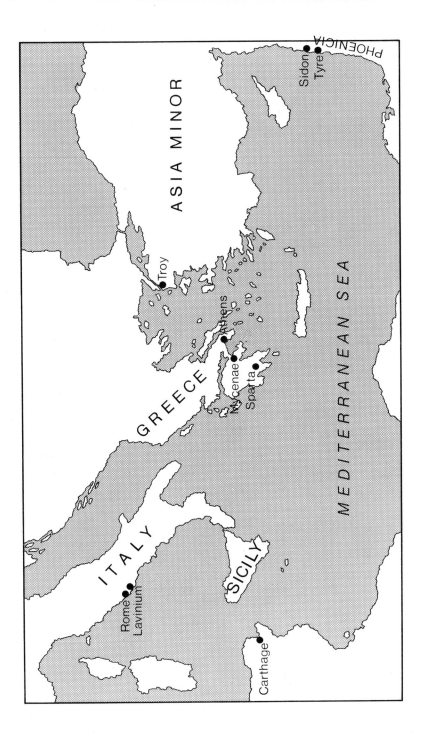

PHOENICIA

Sidon
Tyre

ASIA MINOR

Troy

Athens

GREECE

Mycenae
Sparta

MEDITERRANEAN SEA

ITALY

Rome
Lavinium

SICILY

Carthage

line

1 **cano:** *I sing of*; an appropriate word for an epic poem, which would originally have been chanted. Take **Troiae** with **oris**. In verse, the word order is often varied considerably to meet the demands of the metre. (Cf. **Tyrias . . . arces** in line 8 and **maria omnia circum** in line 16.) In this case, the word order also stresses Troy and Italy, the beginning and end of the journey. **qui primus venit:** *who was the first to come.*

2 **Italiam Lavinaque litora:** Supply **ad** before this phrase. (See LN # 1 for a note explaining the omission of prepositions in verse.) This phrase also contains an example of **-que** used, not to give another piece of information, but to give more information about the first part, *he came to Italy or, to be more precise, to the shores of Lavinium.* (See LN # 37.) Lavinium was the town which Aeneas was to found in Latium. **fato profugus:** literally *exiled by fate*, i.e. *fated to be an exile.*

3 **multum iactatus:** *much buffeted, much tossed about.* **et terris . . . et alto:** a poetical form of **terra marique**, *by land and sea.*

4 **superum = superorum. memorem ob iram:** See lines 7–12 for the reasons for her unrelenting anger.

5 **urbs antiqua:** The city referred to was Carthage. Carthage was a Phoenician colony and Tyre was one of the leading cities of Phoenicia. Under Hannibal, the Carthaginians came close to destroying Rome, but Carthage itself was ultimately captured and destroyed by the Romans. **tenuere:** This alternative form of **tenuerunt** is useful to the poet because of its different metrical form.

6 **unam:** *alone.*

7 **sed enim:** *however.* Note that **sed** has been delayed to second word. **duci:** *was being created* (present infinitive passive as part of accusative and infinitive).

8 **quae verteret:** a purpose clause – (literally) *so that it might overthrow*; translate *which was destined to overthrow.*

9 **necdum:** *and not yet.* **irarum:** In poetry, we frequently find a noun used in the plural with a singular meaning. **saevi dolores:** *bitter resentment*, another example of poetic plural.

10 **alta mente repostum:** *stored up deep in her mind*, i.e. indelibly printed on her memory. Note how the idea "deep" has been transferred from the participle **repostum** to the noun **mente** (Transferred Epithet, LN # 14). **repostum** is a shortened form of **repositum**. Again, the preposition is omitted, as frequently. (Cf. line 2 above.)

·ARRIVAL IN CARTHAGE·

1 The scene is set

Virgil says that his poem is to be about the hero Aeneas and the troubles he had to endure because of Juno's long-standing hatred of the Trojans.

> arma virumque cano, Troiae qui primus ab oris
> Italiam, fato profugus, Lavinaque venit
> litora; multum ille et terris iactatus et alto
> vi superum saevae memorem Iunonis ob iram.
> 5 urbs antiqua fuit (Tyrii tenuere coloni)
> quam Iuno coluit terris magis omnibus unam.
> progeniem sed enim Troiano a sanguine duci
> audierat, Tyrias olim quae verteret arces.
> necdum etiam causae irarum saevique dolores
> 10 exciderant animo; manet alta mente repostum
> iudicium Paridis spretaeque iniuria formae.
> et genus invisum et rapti Ganymedis honores:

---

11 **spretae iniuria formae:** While the gods and goddesses were feasting, the Goddess Strife had thrown a golden apple into their midst. On it were inscribed the words 'For the fairest.' Juno, Venus and Minerva each thought that she should be awarded the apple. Since they could not decide among themselves, Paris, the son of King Priam of Troy, was asked to act as judge. Juno felt deeply insulted when he awarded the apple to Venus who had promised him as his wife the most beautiful woman in Greece – Helen. Translate *the insult involved in the slighting of her beauty*.

12 **rapti Ganymedis honores:** *The honours bestowed upon Ganymede who was carried off* by the eagle to Mount Olympus to be the cup-bearer of Jupiter. Ganymede was a Trojan, and Juno felt that Jupiter should have chosen a Greek.

11

line

13 **his accensa super:** *angered by these thoughts besides.* **super** is used adverbially here. **iactatos . . . arcebat:** *she drove hither and thither.. . . and thus kept them away.*

14 **reliquias Danaum:** *the remnants left by the Greeks.* It was as if the Greeks had made a huge meal of the Trojans, and these few survivors were the scraps which were left over. **Danaum** is the shortened form of **Danaorum.**

17 **tantae molis erat:** The literal meaning of **moles** is *mass* or *heavy weight.* Here the word refers to the 'effort' or 'labour' required to move a big obstruction: literally, *it was (a task) of so great effort.* Translate *so great a task it was.*

19 **spumas salis:** literally *the foam of salt* (**spumas** is poetic plural). Translate *the salt spray.* Note the sound effect produced by the repeated **-s** in these two words, depicting the passage of the ship through the water. (Alliteration and Onomatopoeia: See LN # 33–34.) **aere:** literally *with bronze,* i.e. *with the bronze prows.* Here, the material is used to represent the article which is made from it.

22 **Aeoliam:** Prepositions are often omitted in verse. (Cf. **Italiam** in line 2; **vasto antro** in line 22; **celsa arce** in line 26.)

23 Note how the five spondees of this four-word line depict the mighty struggle to restrain the winds.

24 **imperio premit:** literally *presses back by his command,* i.e. *keeps under his control.* **ac vinclis et carcere frenat:** The words after **ac** explain **imperio premit** in more detail, i.e. how he kept the winds in check. **vinclis et carcere:** literally *with chains and with prison* – two expressions conveying the same idea. (Hendiadys: LN # 27) Translate *with prison chains.*

25 Note how the repetition of the letters 'm' and 'n' produce the moaning sound of the winds howling within the hollow mountain. In the next line, the two words beginning with 'c' suggest the rattling of the bar across the doorway. (Onomatopoeia: LN # 34) **illi:** *they* (the winds).

26 **celsa arce:** See line 22.

27 **sceptra** is poetic plural. (Compare **iras** later in the line, although the plural idea (**animos** and **iras**) may be conveyed by *angry passions.*)

28 **ni faciat:** *if he did not do this.* Although the imperfect would more usually express an unreal condition in present time, the present subjunctive would be used for *if he were to stop doing this.* **ferant** in line 29 completes the condition *they would carry off.*

29 **rapidi:** *swift and destructive.* The root verb is **rapere.** **auras** is poetic plural.

30 **supplex** is used predicatively here – *as a suppliant,* i.e. *asking for help* (see LN # 36).

his accensa super iactatos aequore toto
Troas, reliquias Danaum atque immitis Achilli,
15 arcebat longe Latio; multosque per annos
errabant acti fatis maria omnia circum.
tantae molis erat Romanam condere gentem.

2 Juno seeks help

Persisting in her hatred, Juno persuades the King of the
Winds to let loose a storm to destroy the Trojan fleet.

vix e conspectu Siculae telluris in altum
vela dabant laeti et spumas salis aere ruebant,
20 cum Iuno, aeternum servans sub pectore vulnus,
nimborum in patriam, loca feta furentibus Austris,
Aeoliam venit.   hic vasto rex Aeolus antro
luctantes ventos tempestatesque sonoras
imperio premit ac vinclis et carcere frenat.
25 illi indignantes magno cum murmure montis
circum claustra fremunt.   celsa sedet Aeolus arce
sceptra tenens mollitque animos et temperat iras.
ni faciat, maria ac terras caelumque profundum
quippe ferant rapidi secum, verrantque per auras.
30 ad quem tum Iuno supplex his vocibus usa est:

Postage stamps issued in 1981 to
commemorate the 2000th anniversary of
Virgil's death.

31 **divom** is the shortened form of **divorum**. (Cf. **superum** in line 4 and **Danaum** in line 14.)

32 **tibi dedit:** *has given you power.* **fluctus** is the direct object of both **mulcere** and **tollere**.

34 **Ilium . . . victosque penates:** the **-que** does not mean 'and' but is used to explain **Ilium**, i.e. the new Troy is *represented by* (came *in the form of* the sacred images of the household gods which were carried out of the burning city. (See LN # 37.)

35 **incute vim ventis:** The clipped sounds and the 'v' sounds indicate the violence of the winds. (Onomatopoeia: LN # 34.) **submersas obrue:** Juno does not simply want to see the ships water-logged so that they cannot sail; they must disappear completely to the bottom of the sea.

36 **diversos** agrees with Trojans (understood).

37 **haec:** object of verb of speaking (understood). **contra** is here used adverbially: *in reply.* **tuus** agrees with **labor** in the next line. Supply **est.** **quid optes:** an indirect question depending on **explorare:** all Juno has to do is to make up her mind about what she wants. The use of **labor** suggests that this may be difficult for her.

38 **mihi:** Note the contrast between **tuus** and **mihi.**

39 **dicta:** Supply **sunt.** Note how the repeated use of the letter 'c' in this line depicts the sudden impact of the blow. (Alliteration and Ono-matopoeia: LN # 34.) **conversa cuspide:** not an ablative absolute, but the ablative showing the instrument with which he carried out the act, i.e. using the end of the shaft. **montem impulit in latus: in** is used with the accusative to indicate 'motion towards'. We would more naturally say *struck the mountain* **on** *its side.*

40 **velut agmine facto:** Virgil is fond of similes (LN # 26). Here he likens the winds to an army lining up ready to go on the march.

41 **data:** Supply **est.** **ruunt . . . perflant:** Both of these are historic presents, used to depict vividly the excitement of the scene (LN # 22).

42 **incubuere = incubuerunt.** The use of the perfect tense in the midst of a series of historic presents indicates the suddenness of the action so that it is now an accomplished fact: the winds had settled on the sea. **totum:** Supply **mare.** **sedibus:** poetic plural.

43 **Eurusque Notusque . . . creberque:** -que. . . -que is frequently used in verse where **et. . . et. . .** would be more common in prose. The frequent use of **-que** (eight times in lines 42–46) creates a feeling of speed, excitement and panic.

44 **vastos volvunt:** The alliteration and the spondees in this line help us to feel the surge of the huge waves as they are rolled towards the shore (LN # 33).

"Aeole, (namque tibi divom pater atque hominum rex
et mulcere dedit fluctus et tollere vento)
gens inimica mihi Tyrrhenum navigat aequor,
Ilium in Italiam portans victosque Penates.
35   incute vim ventis submersasque obrue puppes,
aut age diversos et disice corpora ponto."

3 Aeolus lets loose the winds

Aeolus obediently lets loose the winds. The Trojan fleet is
scattered by the storm and some ships are wrecked.

Aeolus haec contra: "tuus, o regina, quid optes,
explorare labor; mihi iussa capessere fas est."
haec ubi dicta, cavum conversa cuspide montem
40   impulit in latus. ac venti, velut agmine facto,
qua data porta ruunt et terras turbine perflant.
incubuere mari, totumque a sedibus imis
una Eurusque Notusque ruunt creberque procellis
Africus, et vastos volvunt ad litora fluctus.

45 **virum = virorum** (cf. **superum** 1.4, **Danaum** 1.14, **divom** 1.31). Again, the rhythm of the line as well as the sound of the words helps to produce a vivid picture; this time the use of dactyls conveys excitement.

47 **incubat:** *settled*, like a hen settling over her brood.

48 **intonuere = intonuerunt.** Compare line 42 for the use of the perfect tense to interrupt the series of historic presents. **poli:** poetic plural – *sky, heaven*, though English does use the expression 'the heavens'. **stridens Aquilone procella:** literally *a storm creaking with the North Wind.* **stridens** depicts the effect on the ships rather than the sound of the storm itself. The ablative **Aquilone** (Ablative of Instrument: LN # 12) indicates the 'weapon' used by the storm. Translate *A howling gale from the north.*

49 **adversa:** Agrees with **procella** – literally *opposing*; translate *(struck) full on.*

50 **franguntur remi:** Note how the shortness of this sentence (like **dat latus** in the next line, and **intonuere poli** two lines earlier) suggests a sudden helplessness. The perfect tense is not used here, since that would suggest that all the oars were broken at the same time. **avertit:** *swung off course.*

51 **dat:** *offered, exposed.* **cumulo:** *in a heap.* The word suggests the build-up of water till the wave towered over the ships like a sheer mountain. There are two unusual features in this line: firstly, the powerful caesura (after **latus**) so early in the line; secondly, ending the line with a single-syllable word (**mons**). The former enables the rest of the line to build up like the massive wave; the second reproduces the effect of the crashing wave.

52 **tres:** *three ships.* Translate the participle **abreptas** actively, *snatched and.*

53 **mari summo:** *on the surface of the water.* (See LN # 1 for the omission of prepositions in verse.) **ab alto:** *from the deep water.*

54 **in brevia et syrtes:** Here, **et** does not mean *and*; rather, it explains what the *shallow places* (**brevia**) are, *namely, the quicksands.* (Cf. the use of **ac** in line 24.) (LN # 37)

55 The spondees produce the effect of the men struggling to keep afloat.

56 **virum:** See line 45. **Troia** is scanned as three syllables: **Tro-i-a.** It is an adjective here.

57 **iam fortis Achatae:** Supply **navem.**

58 **laxis laterum compagibus:** literally *with the slackened joints of their sides*, i.e. they sprang leaks. **omnes:** Supply **naves.**

59 **imbrem** is used poetically here for *sea water.*

45 insequitur clamorque virum stridorque rudentum.
    eripiunt subito nubes caelumque diemque
    Teucrorum ex oculis. ponto nox incubat atra.

4 The storm strikes the fleet

The storm has a devastating effect on the Trojan fleet. The ships are scattered and some of them destroyed.

        intonuere poli.   stridens Aquilone procella
        velum adversa ferit fluctusque ad sidera tollit.
50   franguntur remi.   tum prora avertit et undis
        dat latus.   insequitur cumulo praeruptus aquae mons.
        tres Notus abreptas in saxa latentia torquet,
        dorsum immane mari summo; tres Eurus ab alto
        in brevia et syrtes urget (miserabile visu).
55   apparent rari nantes in gurgite vasto,
        arma virum tabulaeque et Troia gaza per undas.
        iam validam Ilionei navem, iam fortis Achatae,
        vicit hiems; laxis laterum compagibus omnes
        accipiunt inimicum imbrem rimisque fatiscunt.

Neptune

60 **magno misceri murmure pontum:** accusative and infinitive depending on **sensit**. *The sea was being churned up (accompanied) by a great roaring.* Again notice the effect of the repeated "m" (cf. line 25). (Alliteration and Onomatopoeia: LN # 33–34.)

61 **emissam:** Supply **esse**. **alto:** See LN # 1 for the omission of the preposition: *from the deep (i.e. the sea).*

63 **toto aequore:** Which preposition suits best in English?

64 **caelique ruina:** The storm was so violent that it seemed as if the heavens were crashing down on their heads.

65 **nec latuere fratrem:** *did not escape the notice of her brother,* i.e. he knew exactly what Juno was trying to do. **latuere:** The alternative form of **latuerunt** (cf. lines 42 and 48). **irae:** poetic plural.

66 **talia:** *as follows.* **dehinc** is scanned as one syllable: **dēinc**.

67 **generis fiducia vestri:** *confidence in your birth.* Had the fact that they were said to be the sons of Aurora, the Goddess of the Dawn, gone to the heads of the winds and made them over-confident? **tenuit:** *has taken hold of*

68 **numine:** This word is used here in its literal sense of *nodding the head* to show agreement. Translate *divine authority.*

69 **miscere:** *to throw them into utter confusion.* **moles:** See line 17 for this word used in a different context. Here the word refers to the massive waves raised by the storm.

71 **non illi:** Supply **esse** with **datum** and take this infinitive with both **illi** and **mihi**. The accusative and infinitive explains **haec** in more detail.

72 **sorte:** According to Homer, the three brothers Zeus (Jupiter), Poseidon (Neptune) and Hades (Pluto) drew lots to see who would rule the different parts of the universe. Jupiter drew Heaven, Pluto the Underworld and Neptune the Sea. **ille:** *he* (Aeolus).

73 **Eure:** Although addressing only the East Wind by name, Neptune is speaking to all the winds as can be seen from the use of **vestras**. **illa:** Scan the line to see whether the final **-a** is short or long. **se iactet:** present subjunctive to indicate a command: *let him boast.*

74 **clauso carcere:** See LN # 1 for omission of preposition. Note that Neptune emphasises that the prison should be locked, i.e. he should not have let the winds out.

75 **dicto citius:** literally *more quickly than saying it.* (Compare our expression 'Before you could say Jack Robinson.').

77 **Aeneadae:** literally *the sons of Aeneas*, i.e. Aeneas and his followers.

77 **quae proxima:** Supply **sunt** – a relative clause describing **litora**.

78 **vertuntur:** The passive is used here instead of **se vertunt**.

5 Neptune intervenes

Neptune, the God of the Sea, realises there is a storm and takes action to save Aeneas and his fleet.

60   interea magno misceri murmure pontum
       emissamque hiemem sensit Neptunus, et alto
       prospiciens summa placidum caput extulit unda.
       disiectam Aeneae toto videt aequore classem,
       fluctibus oppressos Troas caelique ruina.
65   nec latuere doli fratrem Iunonis et irae.
       Eurum ad se Zephyrumque vocat; dehinc talia fatur:
       "tantane vos generis tenuit fiducia vestri?
       iam caelum terramque meo sine numine, venti,
       miscere et tantas audetis tollere moles?
70   maturate fugam, regique haec dicite vestro:
       non illi imperium pelagi saevumque tridentem,
       sed mihi sorte datum.   tenet ille immania saxa,
       vestras, Eure, domos; illa se iactet in aula
       Aeolus et clauso ventorum carcere regnet."

6 Saved from the storm

Neptune then calms the storm and Aeneas, with his seven remaining ships, heads for the shelter of the nearest shore.

75   sic ait, et dicto citius tumida aequora placat
       collectasque fugat nubes solemque reducit.
       defessi Aeneadae quae proxima litora cursu
       contendunt petere et Libyae vertuntur ad oras.

80 **magno telluris amore:** *with a great longing for (dry) land*, i.e. thankful to have reached land.

81 **Troes:** The final syllable is short. **optata harena:** Remember that **potiri** governs the ablative case.

83 **silici:** *from the flint.*

84 **succepit:** an archaic form of **suscepit.** The leaves were piled underneath to catch the spark from the flint: first leaves, then small twigs, and finally larger pieces of wood. **circum. . .dedit:** the verb has been split into two parts (Tmesis: LN # 28) so that the prefix **circum** is used adverbially: *He placed (more kindling) around (the flame).*

85 **nutrimenta:** poetic plural.

86 **Cererem:** *corn* – the name of the Goddess of Agriculture is substituted for crops she produces – a poetic device. (Metonymy: LN # 31) **Cerealia arma:** *cooking utensils.*

87 **fessi rerum:** literally *weary of things.* Although **rerum** seems to be rather a vague word, it manages to conjure up in one's mind all the troubles and anxieties they had had to face. Translate *though worn-out by all that had happened to them.* **fruges receptas:** *corn they had salvaged.*

90 **Anthea si quem videat: si** here introduces a purpose clause – *to see if.* **Anthea** is accusative case (Greek accusative: LN # 4). Translate *in the hope that he might see some (sign of) Antheus.* Note the alliterative use of the letter 'p' (**prospectum, pelago, petit**). (LN # 33)

92 **Capyn:** accusative of Capys (Greek accusative: LN # 4).
arma: The shields would be slung over the side of the ship to make more room for the rowers. Compare the Norse ships.

94 **armenta:** nominative plural – *all the beasts* or *the whole herd.*

98 **alta:** This adjective is used predicatively, i.e. not *holding their high heads* but *holding their heads high* (LN # 36).

99 **vulgus et omnem turbam:** another example of the explanatory use of **et:** *the common sort*, **namely** *the whole herd* (LN # 37).

100 **miscet:** This verb is used to describe the creating of great confusion. (Cf. line 60 where the sea was being churned up.) When panic set in, the animals ran in all directions, creating the impression of something being stirred up.

101 **prius. . .quam:** Latin frequently splits **priusquam** in this way. (Tmesis: LN # 28) Do not translate **prius** where it appears but take **priusquam** as one word where **quam** appears. By using the subjunctives **fundat** and **aequet** Virgil expresses Aeneas' intention not to stop until he had killed a certain number of animals.

huc septem Aeneas collectis navibus omni
80 ex numero subit. ac magno telluris amore
egressi, optata potiuntur Troes harena
et sale tabentes artus in litore ponunt.
ac primum silici scintillam excudit Achates
succepitque ignem foliis atque arida circum
85 nutrimenta dedit rapuitque in fomite flammam.
tum Cererem corruptam undis Cerealiaque arma
expediunt fessi rerum, frugesque receptas
et torrere parant flammis et frangere saxo.

7 Aeneas goes out to reconnoitre

Aeneas climbs on to a high rock to see if there is any sign
of his lost companions. No luck! But he does get some
welcome food for the seven ships that remain.

Aeneas scopulum interea conscendit et omnem
90 prospectum late pelago petit, Anthea si quem
iactatum vento videat Phrygiasque biremes
aut Capyn aut celsis in puppibus arma Caici.
navem in conspectu nullam, tres litore cervos
prospicit errantes. hos tota armenta sequuntur
95 a tergo, et longum per valles pascitur agmen.
constitit hic, arcumque manu celeresque sagittas
corripuit (fidus quae tela gerebat Achates),
ductoresque ipsos primum, capita alta ferentes
cornibus arboreis, sternit; tum vulgus et omnem
100 miscet agens telis nemora inter frondea turbam.
nec prius absistit quam septem ingentia victor
corpora fundat humi, et numerum cum navibus aequet.

line

103 **in** is used with the accusative to signify the action of handing out the food 'into' their midst. For all that, the most natural translation is *among*. An object must be understood with **partitur**.

104 **deinde:** Take with **vina dividit.**   **onerarat** is a shortened form of **oneraverat**: *had stored*.

106 **neque sumus ante:** The present tense is used with **ante** to indicate a situation which existed in the past and is still continuing in the present: *we have not previously been*.

107 **o passi graviora:** This picks up **o socii** from the previous line: *O you who have suffered worse than this*.   **his quoque finem:** Note the effect of **quoque** – a reassuring word in these circumstances. They have come successfully through worse things than this; why should this be an exception? Note how the pace of the line changes from the weariness at the start of the line to the more cheerful dactyls in which he tries to raise their spirits.

108 **vos:** The repetition of **vos** in lines 108 and 109 is intended to have the same effect as **quoque:** *you* are the same people who came safely through the dangers mentioned in these two lines.   **Scyllaeam rabiem:** Scylla was a notorious rock and Charybdis a whirlpool in the stormy straits between Italy and Sicily.

109 **accestis** is a shortened form of **accessistis**.   **Cyclopea saxa:** Cyclops was the one-eyed monster blinded by Odysseus in his cave near Mount Etna in Sicily.

110 **experti:** Supply **estis**.

111 **et haec:** *even these troubles*. **forsan et haec olim meminisse iuvabit:** a line that every true optimist should learn by heart. Note too the quiet determination displayed in the next two lines – the effect of the repeated **per** and the rhythm of the metre.

112 **tot discrimina rerum:** Compare line 87 for this vague use of **rerum**. He is thinking of the countless factors, known and unknown, which have a hand in determining one's destiny at certain critical moments in one's life. *So many situations in which our fate hung in the balance*.

114 **illic:** After the strong break so early in the line, this word rings out triumphantly.   **fas:** Supply **est**. **fas** comes from the same root as **fari**, to speak.

115 **vosmet:** *yourselves*.   **rebus secundis:** *for more favourable times*.

116 **talia voce refert:** literally *he brought back such things with his voice*, i.e. *thus he spoke*. Note the sharp contrast in lines 116–117 between the outward impression he was trying to create (**voce** and **vultu**) and how he really felt (**corde**). **aeger:** *although sick*.

117 **altum corde: altum** is used predicatively – *deep in his heart*. (LN # 36)

8 A speech to rally flagging spirits

He returns to his friends and, after sharing out the food and
wine, he tries to boost their morale. "We have been
through worse than this and it will all be worthwhile when
we reach the promised land of Latium."

> hinc portum petit et socios partitur in omnes.
> vina, bonus quae deinde cadis onerarat Acestes,
> 105 dividit, et dictis maerentia pectora mulcet:
> "o socii (neque enim ignari sumus ante malorum),
> o passi graviora, dabit deus his quoque finem.
> vos et Scyllaeam rabiem penitusque sonantes
> accestis scopulos; vos et Cyclopea saxa
> 110 experti.   revocate animos maestumque timorem
> mittite!   forsan et haec olim meminisse iuvabit.
> per varios casus, per tot discrimina rerum
> tendimus in Latium, sedes ubi fata quietas
> ostendunt.   illic fas regna resurgere Troiae.
> 115 durate et vosmet rebus servate secundis!"

9 The meal

Slightly encouraged, they cook the venison and, after the
meal, lie down to rest on the shore, all the while wondering
what has happened to their lost companions.

> talia voce refert, curisque ingentibus aeger
> spem vultu simulat, premit altum corde dolorem.
> illi se praedae accingunt dapibusque futuris:
> tergora diripiunt costis et viscera nudant.

---

118 **illi:** *they*, i.e. his companions.   **praedae:** The spoil was the deer
which Aeneas had caught.   **dapibusque:** Another example of **-que**
used, not in the sense of *and*, but to amplify or explain: i.e. the deer
were to become the feast. (Cf. lines 2, 24, 34, 54, 99; LN # 37.)

119 **viscera:** refers to everything under the skin – the flesh as well as the
entrails. Translate *meat*.   **costis:** *from the ribs.*

120 **pars:** *some*, balanced by **alii** in the next line.   **trementia:** Supply **frusta**.

121 **aena:** three syllables: **a-e-na**.

122 **fusi:** *sprawling*.

123 **implentur:** *they took their fill.* The Latin passive verb imitates the Greek middle voice producing the same meaning as **se implent** (LN # 20).   **Bacchi:** Bacchus was the God of Wine. Compare line 86 for the name of a god being used instead of what he represents. (Metonymy: LN # 31.) Translate *of wine*.

124 **exempta:** Supply **est**, *was removed*. Supply **sunt** with **remotae**.

125 **sermone requirunt:** literally *they searched back in their conversation*, i.e. *they talked about*.

126 **inter dubii:** *torn between*. Note that **inter** follows the nouns it governs.   **seu vivere credant:** This is a very condensed expression made up of the following strands:
(a) **seu credant** is an indirect question depending on a notion contained in **dubii:** (*wondering*) *whether they should believe*.
(b) **credant:** is a deliberative subjunctive: *are they to believe?*
(c) **vivere:** (supply **socios**) is an accusative and infinitive depending on **credant**.
seu. . . sive replaces the more usual **utrum. . . an**.

127 This whole line balances **seu vivere credant**. Supply **credant** after **sive**; the remainder of the line is an accusative and infinitive depending on **credant**.   **extrema pati:** literally *that they were suffering the last things they had to suffer*, i.e. death.   **vocatos:** *when called*.

128 **pius:** *noble-hearted*. Virgil regularly calls Aeneas **pius**. **pietas** was a quality greatly admired by the Romans. It encompassed reverence for the gods, respecting and caring for one's parents, affection for one's family, and patriotism.   **Oronti:** Genitive of Orontes; supply **casum**.

129 **secum:** to be taken with **gemit**. All the accusatives in lines 129–130 are the direct objects of **gemit**.

130 **Gyan:** Greek accusative. (Cf. **Capyn** in line 92.) (LN # 4.) **fata:** poetic plural.

131 **volvens:** *turning over in his mind*. The present participle suggests that he had been, and still was, thinking these thoughts. (Cf. the use of **sumus** in line 106.)

133 **quas accesserit oras:** an indirect question depending on **quaerere**. The three infinitives **exire, explorare** and **quaerere** all depend on **constituit**.

135 **bina:** Scan the line to see whether the **-a** is long or short.

120 pars in frusta secant veribusque trementia figunt.
litore aena locant alii flammasque ministrant.
tum victu revocant vires, fusique per herbam
implentur veteris Bacchi pinguisque ferinae.
postquam exempta fames epulis mensaeque remotae,
125 amissos longo socios sermone requirunt
spemque metumque inter dubii, seu vivere credant
sive extrema pati nec iam exaudire vocatos.
praecipue pius Aeneas nunc acris Oronti,
nunc Amyci casum gemit et crudelia secum
130 fata Lyci fortemque Gyan fortemque Cloanthum.

10 The following day

After a restless night, Aeneas decides to go out again to
reconnoitre. From a distance, he sees men building a
magnificent new city.

at pius Aeneas, per noctem plurima volvens,
ut primum lux alma data est, exire locosque
explorare novos, quas vento accesserit oras
quaerere constituit. graditur comitatus Achate,
135 bina manu lato crispans hastilia ferro.
iamque ascendebant collem, qui plurimus urbi
imminet adversasque aspectat desuper arces.
miratur molem Aeneas, magalia quondam,
miratur portas strepitumque et strata viarum.

---

136 **qui plurimus urbi imminet:** *which loomed large over the city.*

138 **molem:** See lines 17 and 69 for previous uses of this word. Here it
probably means *impressive buildings.*

139 **strata viarum:** a poetical variation for **stratas vias**, which cannot be
fitted into the metre. Translate *the paved streets.*

25

line

140 **pars:** See line 120. Here it is followed by another **pars** in line 142 and **alii** in lines 143 and 144. **ducere:** *to build,* the regular word for constructing anything which is long, such as a ditch or city wall.

142 **concludere sulco:** They were marking the area off with a trench, just as we would now peg it off.

143 **portus:** poetic plural.

145 **scaenis:** poetic plural. **futuris:** *which was to be built.*

146 **qualis:** One of the regular ways of introducing a simile (LN # 26). Take **qualis** with **labor** in the next line: *It was just like the hard work which. . .* **rura:** poetic plural. Scan the line to see whether the final **-a** is long or short in **nova** and **florea.**

148 **mella:** poetic plural.

150 **fervet opus:** The constant movement of the bees creates the impression of a liquid coming to the boil.

153 **obtutu haeret defixus in uno:** *stood rooted to the ground concentrating on the sight in front of him;* (literally *stuck fixed in one gaze*).

154 Scan the line to see whether the **-a** endings are long or short.

155 **incessit:** *made her way.* This verb is often used of a ceremonial walk or march. The early caesura adds dignity to the rhythm.

156 **qualis:** Another simile (cf. line 146). *Just like Diana when. . .* The Eurotas, a river in Laconia, and Cynthus, a mountain on Delos, were two of the favourite haunts of Diana.

140 instant ardentes Tyrii, pars ducere muros
molirique arcem et manibus subvolvere saxa,
pars optare locum tecto et concludere sulco.
hic portus alii effodiunt; hinc lata theatris
fundamenta petunt alii immanesque columnas
145 rupibus excidunt, scaenis decora alta futuris.
qualis apes aestate nova per florea rura
exercet sub sole labor, cum gentis adultos
educunt fetus, aut cum liquentia mella
stipant et dulci distendunt nectare cellas;
150 fervet opus, redolentque thymo fragrantia mella.
"o fortunati, quorum iam moenia surgunt!"
Aeneas ait, et fastigia suspicit urbis.

11 Queen Dido appears

Aeneas' mother, Venus, had surrounded him in a veil of
mist so that he was not seen by the Tyrians. As he watches,
Queen Dido approaches looking as radiant as Diana, the
Goddess of Hunting. All the while, she urges on the work.

dum stupet obtutuque haeret defixus in uno,
regina ad templum, forma pulcherrima Dido,
155 incessit, magna iuvenum stipante caterva.
qualis in Eurotae ripis aut per iuga Cynthi

27

line

157 **mille:** Take with **Oreades**.

158 **illa:** *she*, i.e. Diana herself.

159 **deas omnes:** *all the (other) goddesses*, i.e. the nymphs.

160 **talis:** Just as **qualis** frequently marks the opening of a simile, so **talis** regularly marks the end: *Dido was just like that*. (Cf. **talem** later in the line agreeing with **se**.)
se ferebat suggests a certain stately dignity of movement.

161 **per medios:** *through the midst of her followers*.
instans operi: *pressing on with the work*.
regnisque: explanatory **-que** (LN # 37).

162 **foribus divae:** literally *at the doorway of the goddess*. This was not the doorway of the temple, but the entrance to the inner shrine where the goddess herself was assumed to dwell, hence the use of **divae** (Metonymy: LN # 31). This also explains how she was able to be inside the temple *under the central dome* (**media testudine**), and yet only *at the doorway of the shrine*. Note the omission of the prepositions with both **foribus** and **media testudine**. (LN # 1)

163 **saepta:** feminine, agreeing with Dido understood; (cf. **subnixa**).
armis: literally *by arms*, i.e. *by armed guards*. **solio alte subnixa:** literally *supported high up by her throne*, i.e. *enthroned on high* or *seated high on her throne*.

164 **iura:** *rulings*.

165 **partibus aequabat iustis:** *she was sharing out fairly*, where this could be done; otherwise, lots were drawn.

167 **Anthea:** Greek accusative (LN # 4).

168 **aequore:** For the omission of the preposition see LN # 1. (Cf. **alias oras** in the next line.)

169 **penitus:** *far away*.

170 **ipse:** (*Aeneas*) *himself*.

171 **avidi . . . ardebant:** Two words conveying the same idea, as commonly in poetry, thus intensifying the emotion.

172 **res incognita:** *uncertainty*.

173 **dissimulant:** *they stayed out of sight*. **nube cava amicti:** *concealed by the protective mist* which Venus had put around them. It was *hollow* because it formed a kind of shell round them.

174 **introgressi:** Supply **sunt**. Compare **data (est)**. **copia fandi:** Although **fandi** is genitive, translate *an opportunity* to *speak*.

175 **maximus:** Supply **natu** – *the eldest*. **placido pectore:** The literal meaning of **pectus** is *breast*, but it is also used to describe things within the breast: *heart, soul, emotions* and then, because it was thought that the 'mind' was located in the heart, it also came to

exercet Diana choros, quam mille secutae
hinc atque hinc glomerantur Oreades: illa pharetram
fert humero, gradiensque deas supereminet omnes.
160 talis erat Dido, talem se laeta ferebat
per medios, instans operi regnisque futuris.

12 More Trojan survivors

Suddenly some of Aeneas' lost friends appear, surrounded
by Tyrians. Aeneas and Achates are eager to greet them
but decide to wait and see what will happen to them.

tum foribus divae, media testudine templi,
saepta armis solioque alte subnixa resedit.
iura dabat legesque viris, operumque laborem
165 partibus aequabat iustis aut sorte trahebat;
cum subito Aeneas concursu accedere magno
Anthea Sergestumque videt, fortemque Cloanthum
Teucrorumque alios, ater quos aequore turbo
dispulerat, penitusque alias avexerat oras.
170 obstipuit simul ipse, simul percussus Achates
laetitiaque metuque. avidi coniungere dextras
ardebant, sed res animos incognita turbat.
dissimulant et nube cava speculantur amicti.

13 Ilioneus explains

The prisoners are taken into the temple where Dido is
sitting. Ilioneus tells her of the storm and asks for help.
They have not come as enemies.

postquam introgressi et coram data copia fandi,
175 maximus Ilioneus placido sic pectore coepit:

---

mean *thoughts* and *understanding*. Several of these ideas are
contained in the word as used here: translate *with quiet dignity*.
Ilioneus: four syllables – **I-li-on-eus**.

177 **iustitia:** Scan the line to find out the case of this word. **dedit:** *has granted*, i.e. *allowed*; take with both **condere** and **frenare**.

178 **te:** Direct object of **oramus**. **maria omnia:** For the omission of the preposition see LN # 1.

179 **prohibe:** *hold back*, i.e. do not let your people burn the ships.

180 **pio:** See line 128. **propius aspice:** literally *behold more nearly*. There are two notions involved: *spend time in examining more closely* (instead of dismissing out of hand); and, by being willing to spend that time, *show that you are more kindly disposed*.
res nostras: Note the wealth of meaning contained in the vague word **res**. (Cf. lines 87, 112 and 172.)

181 **populare:** In poetry, it is permissible to use the infinitive to express purpose. (Cf. **vertere** in line 182.) **Penates:** *your homes*, since the household gods symbolise the home.

182 **vertere:** *to take back*. **praedas:** poetic plural.

183 **Hesperiam:** literally *the land of the evening star*. **cognomine dicunt:** *call it*.

185 **hic cursus fuit:** literally *this was our course*, i.e. we were sailing there. There are several unfinished lines in the *Aeneid*. It is a very long poem (almost 10 000 lines), and Virgil died before completing it to his satisfaction. He may have left some lines unfinished deliberately for dramatic effect.

186 **subito** is an adjective. **adsurgens Orion:** The rising of this constellation was usually accompanied by storms.

188 **quo alter nec fuit:** literally *than whom another was not*, i.e. *than whom no one was*. **quo** is Ablative of Comparison.

189 **pietate:** This is an Ablative of Respect (see LN # 10), i.e. it indicates by what something is measured or judged (cf. **bello** and **armis**). For the qualities involved in **pietas** see line 128.

190 **vultum demissa:** The participle **demissa** agrees with **Dido**. The accusative case of a noun depending on a participle or adjective is common in Latin poetry. It is an Accusative of Respect, i.e. she was *cast down* (*as far as her expression was concerned*). (LN # 9). Translate *lowering her eyes*.

192 **quis nesciat:** *who could be ignorant?, who could fail to have heard of?*

194 **Saturniaque arva:** like **et** in line 99, **-que** does not mean *and* but *namely*, i.e. it explains where Hesperia is. (LN # 37) *The land of Saturn* is Latium which, according to legend, Saturn, the father of Jupiter, ruled in the Golden Age.

195 **Erycis fines:** *The land of Eryx* was Sicily, Eryx being a mountain there. **optatis:** The short **-i-** shows that this is present indicative

"o regina, novam cui condere Iuppiter urbem
iustitiaque dedit gentes frenare superbas,
Troes te miseri, ventis maria omnia vecti,
oramus: prohibe infandos a navibus ignes!
180 parce pio generi et propius res aspice nostras.
non nos aut ferro Libycos populare Penates
venimus aut raptas ad litora vertere praedas.
est locus (Hesperiam Grai cognomine dicunt),
terra antiqua, potens armis atque ubere glaebae;
185 hic cursus fuit,
cum subito adsurgens fluctu nimbosus Orion
dispulit. huc pauci vestris adnavimus oris.
rex erat Aeneas nobis, quo iustior alter
nec pietate fuit, nec bello maior et armis."

14 Dido reassures them

Dido bids them welcome. She says she has heard of the
glory of Troy and offers to help them on their way or, if
they prefer it, they may settle in Carthage. She also prom-
ises to send out a search party to look for Aeneas.

190 tum breviter Dido vultum demissa profatur:
"solvite corde metum, Teucri, secludite curas!
quis genus Aeneadum, quis Troiae nesciat urbem
virtutesque virosque aut tanti incendia belli?
seu vos Hesperiam magnam Saturniaque arva
195 sive Erycis fines regemque optatis Acesten,
auxilio tutos dimittam opibusque iuvabo.

---

and not perfect participle. Take this verb with both the **seu** and the
sive clause. **Acesten** is Greek accusative (LN # 4). (Cf. lines 92
and 130.) Acestes was a king in Sicily who had helped the Trojans.
regem is used predicatively: *as king* (LN # 36).

196 **tutos:** Agrees with **vos** (understood from lines 194–195).

197 **vultis et:** *or if you wish.*

198 **urbem quam statuo vestra est: urbs**, the natural subject of **est**, has been attracted into the same case as the relative pronoun **quam**.

199 **mihi:** *by me* – Dative of agent (LN # 7).

200 **utinam Aeneas adforet:** *would that (I wish that) Aeneas were here.* **adforet** is another form of the imperfect subjunctive **adesset**. Used with the imperfect subjunctive, **utinam** expresses a wish that something were true at the present time. **Noto eodem:** Here **Notus** is not specifically the South Wind, but any wind. Translate *by the same wind*, i.e. as brought you here.

201 **certos:** *trusty men.*

203 **si quibus silvis errat:** *in case he is wandering in some woods.* **eiectus:** *thrown out (by the sea),* i.e. *cast ashore.*

204 **animum arrecti:** literally *straightened up as far as their minds were concerned.* Translate *encouraged* or *cheered up.* (Cf. line 190 for the Accusative of Respect, LN # 9.)

205 **pater:** another of the titles given to Aeneas – *father* in the sense of *lord* or *leader.* (Cf. **pius Aeneas** in line 128.) **iamdudum ardebant:** The imperfect tense is used here to describe something that was, and still continued to be, the case: *had long been eager.* (Cf. the present tenses used in lines 106 and 131; and LN # 21.)

207 **nate dea:** A stock way of addressing Aeneas: literally *born from a goddess,* i.e. *O son of the goddess.* Aeneas was the son of Venus. **animo:** See LN # 1 for the omission of the preposition.

209 **unus abest:** The helmsman Orontes had been swept overboard in the storm.

210 **respondent cetera: cetera** is neuter plural and is subject of **respondent** which in this context means *agree* or *confirm.* Venus had promised that all would be well and her words had come true.

212 **scindit se et purgat:** Take **se** with both verbs. **aethera** is a Greek accusative. (Cf. **Anthea** in line 167.)

213 **restitit:** *stood there.*

214 **os umerosque:** Both are Accusatives of Respect (LN # 9). (Cf. line 204.)

216 **adflarat:** shortened form of **adflaverat.** (Cf. **onerarat** in 104.) Literally, the word means *had breathed upon.* The word is suitable for *grace and charm* (**honores**), but less suitable for **caesariem** and **lumen.** In English, either use different verbs with the latter (e.g. *had given* and *had put*) or use a verb like *bestow* for all three. (Zeugma: LN # 29.) **honores:** poetic plural.

218 **improvisus:** literally *un-fore-seen,* i.e. no one had expected it: translate *to everyone's surprise.*

vultis et his mecum pariter considere regnis,
urbem quam statuo vestra est. subducite naves!
Tros Tyriusque mihi nullo discrimine agetur.
200 atque utinam rex ipse, Noto compulsus eodem,
adforet Aeneas! equidem per litora certos
dimittam et Libyae lustrare extrema iubebo,
si quibus eiectus silvis aut urbibus errat.''

15 Aeneas reveals himself

Aeneas and Achates are heartened by these words. The veil
of mist suddenly lifts and reveals them to the others.
Looking like a god, he tells Dido who he is.

his animum arrecti dictis, et fortis Achates
205 et pater Aeneas iamdudum erumpere nubem
ardebant. prior Aenean compellat Achates:
''nate dea, quae nunc animo sententia surgit?
omnia tuta vides, classem sociosque receptos.
unus abest, medio in fluctu quem vidimus ipsi
210 submersum; dictis respondent cetera matris.''
vix ea fatus erat, cum circumfusa repente
scindit se nubes et in aethera purgat apertum.
restitit Aeneas claraque in luce refulsit
os umerosque deo similis; namque ipsa decoram
215 caesariem nato genetrix lumenque iuventae
purpureum et laetos oculis adflarat honores:
tum sic reginam adloquitur cunctisque repente
improvisus ait: ''coram, quem quaeritis, adsum
Troius Aeneas, Libycis ereptus ab undis.

---

219 **Troius:** Three syllables. (Cf. **Troia** in line 56.) The position at the
start of the line makes it sound like a trumpet call – a declaration
of patriotic pride.

220 **o sola miserata:** *o you who alone have pitied.* (**miserata** is the perfect participle, used almost like a noun. Compare **o passi graviora** in line 107.)

221 **di** and **mens** are joint subjects of **ferant** (line 223). **si qua:** neuter plural agreeing with **numina:** *if there are any divine powers which.*

222 **iustitiae:** partitive genitive with **si quid:** *if there is any justice.* **mens sibi conscia recti:** a difficult phrase to translate succinctly because of the wealth of meaning it contains. It is more than *conscience* which can often be taken as almost a negative influence, i.e. it counteracts one's initial reaction. Here it is much more positive – a feeling of well-being which comes from knowing within oneself (**sibi conscia**) that what one is doing is right whatever the world may think. **recti** is genitive with **conscia**. Translate *inner confidence that you have acted honourably.*

223 **ferant:** present subjunctive expressing a wish – *may (they) bring.* **quae te iam laeta tulerunt saecula?:** *What happy world produced* (literally *bore*) *you?*

224 **qui tanti talem genuere parentes?** *What mighty* (**tanti**) *parents gave birth to such a fine person as you* (**talem**)? **genuere = genuerunt** (from **gignere**).

225–6 For the sentiment expressed in these lines compare Robert Burns' promise of eternal love in 'My Love is like a Red, Red Rose':

> 'And I will love thee still, my dear,
> Till a' the seas gang dry.'

montibus: For the omission of the preposition see LN # 1.
dum umbrae lustrabunt convexa: *while the shadows sweep over the hollows.*

227 **laudes:** poetic plural.

228 **quae . . . cunque:** Take together as one word (Tmesis: LN # 28).

229 **Ilionea** is the Greek accusative of **Ilioneus**; it contains five syllables. (See also line 175.) Scan the line to see whether the final **-a** is long or short in **dextra** and **laeva**.

230 **post:** an adverb, not a preposition – *afterwards, and then.* **Gyan:** See line 130.

231 **primo:** Although this is an adjective agreeing with **aspectu**, English would more naturally treat it adverbially – *firstly*. It is balanced by **deinde.** **Sidonia:** one of the regular adjectives applied to Dido because she was a refugee from Sidon.

232 **casu tanto:** *at his great (mis)fortune*, balancing **primo aspectu.**

233 **quis casus:** *what fate.*

234 **immanibus:** *wild, uncivilised* – the Tyrians had only recently settled there.

220   o sola infandos Troiae miserata labores,
      di tibi, si qua pios respectant numina, si quid
      usquam iustitiae est, et mens sibi conscia recti
      praemia digna ferant. quae te iam laeta tulerunt
      saecula? qui tanti talem genuere parentes?
225   in freta dum fluvii current, dum montibus umbrae
      lustrabunt convexa, polus dum sidera pascet,
      semper honos nomenque tuum laudesque manebunt,
      quae me cunque vocant terrae." sic fatus amicum
      Ilionea petit dextra, laevaque Serestum,
230   post alios, fortemque Gyan fortemque Cloanthum.

16 A welcome from Dido

Dido marvels at his appearance although she has heard of
his divine descent. She says she has heard all about the fate
of Troy from a Greek called Teucer who had come to
Sidon, her previous home, asking for help. As one who has
suffered much herself, she is only too willing to help others
in distress.

      obstipuit primo aspectu Sidonia Dido,
      casu deinde viri tanto, et sic ore locuta est:
      "quis te, nate dea, per tanta pericula casus
      insequitur? quae vis immanibus applicat oris?
235   tune ille Aeneas, quem Dardanio Anchisae
      alma Venus Phrygii genuit Simoentis ad undam?

---

235 **tune:** Supply **es.** **Dardanio Anchisae:** *to Trojan Anchises* (see
LDOT 52). Compare the use of **Sidonia** with **Dido** in line 231. Note
that the **–o** is not elided (only three times in the whole poem did
Virgil allow himself this licence, and each time it involved the use of a
proper name), and the second last foot of this line is a spondee ($--$)
instead of the usual dactyl ($-\smile\smile$).

236 **Phrygii Simoentis:** The Simois was a small river in Phrygia, near
Troy. Note again the use of the 'geographical' adjective to add
colour. (Cf. lines 231 and 235.)

237 **Teucrum:** Teucer was a Greek hero who, having been expelled by his father, came to Sidon to ask help from Dido's father, Belus, in the founding of a new state.   **Sidona:** Greek accusative of Sidon (cf. lines 167 and 229.)

239 **genitor:** *my father.*

240 **dicione tenebat:** literally *he was holding it by his authority;* translate *he held it under his sway.* Teucer was helped to settle in Cyprus where he founded a new city which he called Salamis after the city from which he had been expelled.

241 **cognitus:** Supply **est.**

243 Take **o** with **iuvenes** as a parenthesis.

244–5 The word order is quite complex, but the translation should not be difficult provided close attention is paid to the case endings.

245 **hac terra:** For the omission of prepositions see LN # 1.

246 **non ignara:** The double negative produces a strong positive statement – *since I know about.*   **disco:** *I am learning how (to).*

247 **Aenean:** Greek accusative. (Cf. lines 92 and 130.)

248 **divom:** See line 31.   **indicit honorem:** *orders a thank-offering to be made.*

249 **nec minus:** *also.*

250 **magnorum . . . suum: suum** is genitive plural of **sus.**

252 **splendida:** Scanning the line shows that this is nominative case agreeing with **domus.** It is used predicatively (LN # 36): *(was being decorated) splendid(ly).*

253 **mediis tectis:** *in the central hall.*
convivia and **tectis** are both poetic plurals.

254–7 Supply **sunt,** *there were,* with this whole passage.

254 **ostro superbo:** The purple is described as *proud* because of its association with royalty.

255 **caelata in auro fortia facta patrum:** *the brave deeds of ancestors wrought in gold.* The history of the race was told in the scenes engraved in the gold cups.

257 **per tot ducta viros:** *traced through so many (i.e. countless) generations.*

258 **patrius amor:** *a father's love (for his son).*

259 **passus:** Supply **est.**   **Achaten:** See lines 92, 130 and 247.
rapidum is used predicatively (LN # 36): *sent him speeding.*

260 **ferat:** Treat as a purpose clause. Translate *(he sent Achates) to carry.* Treat **ducat** in the same way.   **haec:** *these tidings, this news.*
ipsum: i.e. Ascanius.

atque equidem Teucrum memini Sidona venire,
finibus expulsum patriis, nova regna petentem
auxilio Beli; genitor tum Belus opimam
240 vastabat Cyprum et victor dicione tenebat.
tempore iam ex illo casus mihi cognitus urbis
Troianae nomenque tuum regesque Pelasgi.
quare agite, o tectis iuvenes succedite nostris!
me quoque per multos similis fortuna labores
245 iactatam hac demum voluit consistere terra.
non ignara mali, miseris succurrere disco."

17 Food and gifts for Aeneas' companions

She invites Aeneas into the palace and offers sacrifice to the
gods. She prepares a banquet for her guests and sends large
quantities of food to their friends at the ships.

sic memorat.　simul Aenean in regia ducit
tecta, simul divom templis indicit honorem.
nec minus interea sociis ad litora mittit
250 viginti tauros, magnorum horrentia centum
terga suum, pingues centum cum matribus agnos.
at domus interior regali splendida luxu
instruitur, mediisque parant convivia tectis:
arte laboratae vestes ostroque superbo,
255 ingens argentum mensis caelataque in auro
fortia facta patrum, series longissima rerum
per tot ducta viros antiqua ab origine gentis.

18 Achates is sent to fetch Ascanius

Aeneas is anxious about his son, Ascanius, and sends
Achates to fetch him and also to bring gifts for the queen.

Aeneas (neque enim patrius consistere mentem
passus amor) rapidum ad naves praemittit Achaten,
260 Ascanio ferat haec, ipsumque ad moenia ducat;

261 **omnis cura:** *every thought.* **stat:** *rested, centred.*

263 **signis auroque:** literally *with markings and gold,* i.e. *with gold embroidery.* (Hendiadys: LN # 27) There was so much embroidery that it was stiff.

264 **acantho:** i.e. with the design of acanthus leaves.

265 **ornatus** is accusative plural in apposition to **pallam** and **velamen. Argivae** and **Mycenis:** These words are used rather loosely by Virgil. Menelaus, Helen's husband, was actually King of Sparta and it was from there that she fled with Paris. The King of Mycenae was Agamemnon, the brother of Menelaus. Since he was leader of the whole expedition, however, it seems reasonable to say she brought the garments *from Mycenae.* Argos was a town in the Peloponnese (near Mycenae) with which both Agamemnon and Menelaus were associated, but here the adjective **Argivae** means little more than *Greek.*

266 **peteret:** Note that the final syllable is regarded as long because it comes immediately before the caesura. **inconcessos hymenaeos:** the *unlawful marriage* was to Paris. By leaving her husband and running off with Paris, Helen was responsible for the Trojan War. **hymenaeos** is poetic plural.

267 **extulerat:** The subject is **illa,** *she.* **donum** is in apposition to **ornatus.**

268 **Ilione:** nominative (Greek).

269 **maxima:** *eldest.* (Cf. line 175.) **collo monile: collo** is dative – literally *a collar for the neck,* i.e. *a necklace.*

271 **haec celerans:** *carrying out these orders swiftly.* **iter tendebat:** *made his way.*

272 **Cytherea:** *Venus,* so called after the Aegean island, Cythera, famed for her worship. (Cf. line 282.) **pectore:** See line 175 for the various meanings of **pectus.**

273 **ut Cupido veniat:** Purpose clause. **faciem mutatus et ora:** Accusative of Respect (see LN # 9, and cf. lines 190, 204, and 214) – *changed in form and features.*

274 **furentem** anticipates what is to happen to her: *kindle her to madness.*

275 **ossibus implicet ignem:** The fire is the fire of love and, since the feelings were thought to reside in the marrow of the bones, it was not surprising that one of Cupid's particular targets should be to *wrap the fire within her bones.*

277 **solus** is in apposition to **nate** – *O son, you who alone (are my strength).*

omnis in Ascanio cari stat cura parentis.
munera praeterea Iliacis erepta ruinis
ferre iubet, pallam signis auroque rigentem
et circumtextum croceo velamen acantho,
265 ornatus Argivae Helenae, quos illa Mycenis,
Pergama cum peteret inconcessosque hymenaeos,
extulerat, matris Ledae mirabile donum;
praeterea sceptrum, Ilione quod gesserat olim,
maxima natarum Priami, colloque monile
270 bacatum et duplicem gemmis auroque coronam.
haec celerans iter ad naves tendebat Achates.

The top of a Corinthian column showing
the design of acanthus leaves.

19 Venus intervenes

But Venus, who wants Aeneas to settle in Carthage and
marry Dido, decides to substitute Cupid, the God of Love,
for Ascanius to help win the affections of Dido.

at Cytherea novas artes, nova pectore versat
consilia, ut faciem mutatus et ora Cupido
pro dulci Ascanio veniat donisque furentem
275 incendat reginam atque ossibus implicet ignem.
ergo his aligerum dictis adfatur Amorem:
"nate, meae vires, mea magna potentia solus,

278 **supplex:** Compare line 30 for this word used predicatively. (LN # 36)

279 **regius:** Take with **puer** – *prince*.

280 **mea maxima cura** is in apposition to **puer**.

281 **restantia:** literally *remaining*, i.e. *saved*.

282 **hunc:** *him*, direct object of **recondam**.

284 **ne qua:** *lest* (*in case*) *in some way*. The subject of **possit** is Ascanius. **medius occurrere:** literally *come upon it in the middle*, i.e. *stumble into the middle of it*. **medius** agrees with the subject of the sentence. **dolos:** poetic plural.

285 **non amplius unam:** *no more than one*. The omission of **quam** with numerals is normal Latin. **faciem illius falle dolo:** literally *pretend his appearance by guile*, i.e. *disguise yourself and impersonate him*.

286 **vultus:** poetic plural.

288 **regales inter mensas:** *amidst the royal feast*, the tables standing for what was placed on them. **laticem Lyaeum:** literally *the Lyaean liquid*, i.e. 'wine' since Lyaeus was one of the titles of Bacchus, God of Wine.

290 **occultum ignem:** the *hidden fire* and the *poison* (**veneno**) both refer to the passionate love for Aeneas which Cupid is going to implant in her. **inspires** and **fallas** are both subjunctive, being the verbs of the purpose clause which began with **ut** in line 287. **fallas** contains the idea of doing something without its being noticed: *poison her unawares*.

292 **gressu gaudens:** Cupid was renowned for enjoying pranks. It is also a novelty for him to be walking instead of flying.

Dido receiving Aeneas and Cupid,
who has been substituted for
Aeneas' son, Ascanius. (Painting by
Francesco Solimena)

ad te confugio et supplex tua numina posco.
regius accitu cari genitoris ad urbem
280 Sidoniam puer ire parat, mea maxima cura,
dona ferens pelago et flammis restantia Troiae;
hunc ego sopitum somno super alta Cythera
aut super Idalium sacrata sede recondam,
ne qua scire dolos mediusve occurrere possit.
285 tu faciem illius noctem non amplius unam
falle dolo et notos pueri puer indue vultus,
ut, cum te gremio accipiet laetissima Dido
regales inter mensas laticemque Lyaeum,
cum dabit amplexus atque oscula dulcia figet,
290 occultum inspires ignem fallasque veneno."
paret Amor dictis carae genetricis, et alas
exuit et gressu gaudens incedit Iuli.

41

line

293 **at:** *on the other hand.* **Ascanio** is a dative which has the force of a genitive.

294 **inrigat:** a metaphor drawn from the irrigation of the fields: the drowsiness comes over him slowly, like the slow movement of the water in the irrigation ditches. **fotum gremio: fotum** (which is the perfect participle passive of **foveo**) agrees with **Ascanium** or **eum** (understood). Translate *holding him close to her.* **dea** is used predicatively (LN # 36): *as only a goddess could.*

296 **floribus et umbra** should be taken with **adspirans:** literally *breathing on him with its flowers and pleasant shade.*

297 **dicto parens:** *obeying his instructions.*

298 **duce laetus Achate:** literally *joyful, Achates being the guide,* i.e. *happy to be led along by Achates.*

299 **iuventus:** not *young men* but *men in their prime* (roughly 18–45 years of age, according to the Romans). Translate *men.*

300 **discumbitur** is an impersonal passive: *places were taken,* i.e. *they reclined.* **strato super ostro**: *on the purple-covered couches.*

301 **Cererem:** *bread,* another example of Metonymy (LN # 31).

302 **tonsis villis** is an Ablative of Description (LN # 11). Since the nap of the towels was close-cut, they would be soft.

303 **nec non et:** . . . *also.*

304 **convenere** = **convenerunt.** **iussi:** The Queen had ordered them to attend the feast. **pictis:** not *painted,* but *embroidered.*

305 **Iulum:** In lines 260 and 274, Aeneas' son was called Ascanius. Here, his other name – Iulus – is used. Remember, however, that it is not really Iulus who is at the banquet but Cupid who is impersonating him; hence the reference to **dei** in the next line.

306 **flagrantes:** *radiant.* **simulata:** because they were spoken by the god, not by Iulus.

308 **infelix:** not *unhappy* because she was obviously enjoying the evening but rather *luckless* because of the misfortune it would bring upon her later and the confused emotions she was experiencing. *Poor* comes very close to capturing all these ideas. **pesti devota:** *condemned to destruction.* She was to commit suicide when Aeneas deserted her.

309 **expleri mentem: mentem** is an Accusative of Respect (LN # 9), *to be satisfied as far as her heart was concerned.* Translate *to satisfy her passion.* **tuendo:** ablative of gerund – *with gazing.*

311 **ille:** Cupid (alias Iulus). **complexu colloque:** English requires two different prepositions: literally *hung on his embrace and from his neck.* Translate *had hung with his arms clasped round his neck.*

at Venus Ascanio placidam per membra quietem
inrigat et fotum gremio dea tollit in altos
295 Idaliae lucos, ubi mollis amaracus illum
floribus et dulci adspirans complectitur umbra.
iamque ibat dicto parens et dona Cupido
regia portabat Tyriis duce laetus Achate.

20 Cupid's mission succeeds

After the gifts have been handed over, the Tyrians and
their guests begin their meal. Cupid sets about the task of
making Dido fall in love with Aeneas.

iam pater Aeneas et iam Troiana iuventus
300 conveniunt, stratoque super discumbitur ostro.
dant manibus famuli lymphas, Ceremque canistris
expediunt, tonsisque ferunt mantelia villis.
nec non et Tyrii per limina laeta frequentes
convenere, toris iussi discumbere pictis.
305 mirantur dona Aeneae, mirantur Iulum
flagrantesque dei vultus simulataque verba,
pallamque et pictum croceo velamen acantho.
praecipue infelix, pesti devota futurae,
expleri mentem nequit ardescitque tuendo
310 Phoenissa, et pariter puero donisque movetur.
ille ubi complexu Aeneae colloque pependit,

A large Greek **crater** or
wine bowl (see line 320).
This one is made of
bronze. It was found
during the excavation of a
tomb at Vix, in France. It
stands over one and a half
metres high and weighs
over two hundred
kilograms.

312 **falsi:** *false* or *deluded*, because Cupid was pretending to be his son. Or translate *his father who was not his father.*

313 **haec:** *she* (Dido).

314 **gremio fovet:** *fondled him on her lap, cuddled him.* **inscia:** The indirect question **quantus deus miserae insidat** depends on this adjective.

315 **miserae** agrees with 'her' (understood): *was taking possession of her, wretched woman that she was.*

316 **matris Acidaliae:** *of his Acidalian mother*, i.e. *of Venus.* She was said to bathe at the Acidalian Fountain in Boeotia.
Sychaeum: Sychaeus had been Dido's husband. Dido's brother murdered him for his wealth and Dido fled from Tyre for safety.

317 **vivo:** a *living* love, contrasted with her *sleeping* (**resides**) love for Sychaeus: she had forgotten what it was like to be in love. **praevertere:** *to take possession of before she realised what was happening*, i.e. *to take by surprise.* **animos** and **corda** are poetic plurals.

319 **prima quies:** Supply **fuit**; also **sunt** with **remotae**.

320 **crateras:** These were big wine bowls in which the wine was diluted with water before being served. We get the English word 'crater' straight from this word. **vina coronant: vina** is poetic plural. *They put garlands round the (bowls of) wine.*

321 **tectis:** poetic plural, and see LN # 1 for omission of preposition. **strepitus** describes the noise of a large company of people holding several conversations at the same time. **crinitus Iopas:** It was customary to have a minstrel sing songs, particularly heroic tales, after a banquet.

322 **personat:** *he made (the palace) resound.* **Atlas** was the Titan who was compelled to hold up the heavens on his shoulders. In later legend he became a wise old philosopher.

323 **ingeminant plausu:** literally *redouble with applause* – a poetic way of saying *redoubled their applause.*

324 **nec non et:** Compare line 303. **trahebat:** *prolonged*, i.e. made the evening last longer because she did not wish Aeneas to leave.

325 **infelix:** Cf. line 308.

326 **multa:** The repetition of **multa** and the repetitive form of the verb **rogitare** describe how she kept the conversation going by asking question after question. Compare the triple use of **nunc** in the next two lines.

327 **quibus . . . armis** is an indirect question depending on **rogitans**. **Aurorae filius:** Memnon, King of the Ethiopians, who fought for the Trojans but was killed by Achilles. His arms had been made for him by the god Vulcan.

et magnum falsi implevit genitoris amorem,
reginam petit. haec oculis, haec pectore toto
haeret, et interdum gremio fovet, inscia Dido,
315 insidat quantus miserae deus. at memor ille
matris Acidaliae paulatim abolere Sychaeum
incipit, et vivo temptat praevertere amore
iam pridem resides animos desuetaque corda.

21 After the meal

After the meal they talk together and listen to a minstrel.
Dido has become so infatuated with Aeneas that she tries
to keep the conversation going till far into the night by
asking him all about the siege of Troy.

postquam prima quies epulis mensaeque remotae,
320 crateras magnos statuunt et vina coronant.
it strepitus tectis.   cithara crinitus Iopas
personat aurata, docuit quem maximus Atlas.
ingeminant plausu Tyrii, Troesque sequuntur.
nec non et vario noctem sermone trahebat
325 infelix Dido longumque bibebat amorem,
multa super Priamo rogitans, super Hectore multa;
nunc quibus Aurorae venisset filius armis,
nunc quales Diomedis equi, nunc quantus Achilles.
"immo age, et a prima dic, hospes, origine nobis
330 insidias" inquit "Danaum casusque tuorum
erroresque tuos; nam te iam septima portat
omnibus errantem terris et fluctibus aestas."

---

328 **Diomedis equi:** In her eagerness to ask questions, Dido had obviously forgotten that these famous horses had been won from Aeneas by Diomedes in a chariot-race.

329 **immo age et dic:** *rather, instead (of dealing with the stories piecemeal) come, tell us* the whole story.

330 **tuorum:** *of your own people.* **Danaum:** Genitive plural (cf. line 14).

331 **errores tuos:** Since the fall of Troy, Aeneas had spent more than six years searching for Hesperia.

1 **conticuere** = **conticuerunt:** The perfect tense suggests that it happened suddenly: *fell silent.* **intenti:** literally *stretched*, referring probably to their minds, i.e. *attentive* or, more naturally, *attentively.* **ora tenebant:** *checked their speech*, i.e. *kept quiet.*

2 **pater Aeneas:** One of the titles given to Aeneas – *father* in the sense of *lord* or *leader.* **orsus:** Supply **est.**

3 **infandum:** Note the emphasis given to this word by placing it first in the sentence and **dolorem** last. **iubes:** Supply **me.**

4 **si tantus amor:** Supply **est tibi** (literally *is to you*, i.e. *you have).* **casus:** The plural of a noun is often used in poetry where a singular would be used in prose (LN # 2).

5 **luctu refugit:** The long **-u-** of **refugit** shows that this is the perfect tense. This tense shows how suddenly he reacted to the request (his initial reaction being to refuse), whereas the present tense of **horret** describes his continuing unease.

7 **Danaum** = **Danaorum** (LN # 5). **tot iam labentibus annis:** The present tense of this ablative absolute indicates that the years had been, and still were, slipping past. It was the tenth year of the siege.

8 **instar montis:** literally *the image of a mountain*, i.e. *as high as a mountain.* The phrase is in apposition to **equum.** **Palladis arte:** Pallas Athene, the Goddess of Arts and Crafts, supported the Greeks against the Trojans whom she hated because the Trojan prince, Paris, had judged Venus more beautiful than herself. (See Arrival in Carthage line 11.)

9 **milite:** *with a company of soldiers* (singular used collectively – LN # 3).

10 **Tenedos** is an island off the coast of Troas, the area round Troy. **notissima fama insula:** By scanning the lines we discover that the final **-a-** of **notissima** and **insula** is short. Being the final syllable in the line, the final **-a-** of **fama** could be either long or short; however, since **insula** is nominative, **fama** must be ablative, denoting the respect in which the island is held.

11 **dives opum:** The genitive is common after adjectives expressing fullness or emptiness. Translate *rich in resources.* **dum:** *while* in the sense of *as long as.* **regna:** poetic plural, but the word *realms* is available in English.

12 **sinus:** Supply **est.** **tantum** means *only.* **statio:** literally *a place to stand.* i.e. *an anchorage* rather than a harbour. **male fida:** When **male** is attached to an adjective denoting a good quality, it has the effect of producing the opposite of that quality: *not trustworthy*, i.e. *treacherous.* **carinis:** Strictly speaking, the **carina** was the keel of the ship, but frequently Virgil uses a word denoting part of a ship to stand for the ship itself: translate *ships.* (Synecdoche: part standing for whole: LN # 32)

13 **se** is to be taken with **condunt** – *concealed themselves.*

·THE LAST DAYS OF TROY·

1 Aeneas agrees to tell the story

Aeneas, in his flight from Troy, has reached Carthage where he is welcomed by Queen Dido. When the feasting is over, Dido asks Aeneas to tell her the sad story of the destruction of Troy by the Greeks.

> conticuere omnes, intentique ora tenebant.
> inde toro pater Aeneas sic orsus ab alto:
> 'infandum, regina, iubes renovare dolorem;
> sed si tantus amor casus cognoscere nostros,
> 5 quamquam animus meminisse horret luctuque refugit,
> incipiam.

2 The story begins

The siege of Troy had already lasted for ten years when the Greeks hit on the stratagem of the wooden horse and then sailed for the island of Tenedos.

> fracti bello fatisque repulsi,
> ductores Danaum, tot iam labentibus annis,
> instar montis equum divina Palladis arte
> aedificant, uterumque armato milite complent.
> 10 est in conspectu Tenedos, notissima fama
> insula, dives opum, Priami dum regna manebant:
> nunc tantum sinus et statio male fida carinis.
> huc se provecti deserto in litore condunt.

47

14 **nos abiisse rati:** Supply **eos** with **abiisse** and **sumus** with **rati.**
petiisse continues the accusative and infinitive. **vento:** An Ablative
of Instrument, i.e. what they used to get there. Translate *before the
wind* (LN # 12). **Mycenas:** Agamemnon, leader of the Greeks,
was King of Mycenae. Here it symbolises Greece.

15 A very effective line. The spondees suggest the weariness of the long
siege. Note too how the two adjectives (**omnis** and **longo**) are set side
by side near the beginning, and the two nouns with which they agree
(**Teucria** and **luctu**) at the end. **Teucria:** literally *the land of
Teucer:* i.e. *Troy.* Teucer was one of the early kings of Troy.

16 **panduntur portae:** The change in rhythm after these words shows the
sudden excitement and happiness. **iuvat:** an impersonal verb – *it
gave (us) pleasure.* **et** links **ire** and **videre**; **-que** (used twice) links
the three direct objects. **Dorica:** one of the many names used for
Greek. (See page 122.)

17 **locos:** *positions* where troops had been stationed.

18 In this line and the next, the Trojans point out various places to each
other as they wander around. **tendebat:** literally *stretched (his tent),*
i.e. *made camp.* Note that both **manus** and **Achilles** are subjects of
this verb.

19 **locus:** Supply **erat.** The ships would have been pulled up on to the
shore. **solebant:** i.e. the soldiers of both sides. **acie:** Prepositions
are frequently omitted in verse. (See LN # 1.)

20 **pars:** *some* (of the Trojans). **donum Minervae: Minervae** is genitive;
it could have two senses – *the gift which she had given* or *the gift given
to her.* In this line it is the latter: the horse had been left as an
offering to her. Translate *the gift left for Minerva* (LN # 6). Minerva
was the name which the Romans gave to Pallas Athene.

21 **moles:** See AIC line 17 for a discussion of the meaning of this word.
Here it refers to the *massive bulk* of the horse. **mirantur:** The verb
is plural continuing the idea of **pars,** *some.* **primus:** Very emphatic
position – *was the first to.* **Thymoetes** had a grudge against Priam
because the latter had had the wife and child of Thymoetes put to
death to satisfy an oracle. This explains the use of **dolo** in line 23,
although he is given the benefit of the doubt – **sive dolo seu fata
ferebant,** i.e. he may have been the victim of fate.

22 **duci hortatur:** *urged that it be brought*; the passive infinitive (in place
of **ut** + subjunctive) is normal Latin even with a verb like **hortatur.**
arce: For the omission of the preposition see LN # 1. The **arx** was
not simply inside the city, but inside the inner fortress.

23 **sive dolo . . . ferebant:** The notion of *because of treachery* (literally
from) leads one's thoughts quite naturally along to *or (because). . .*
in the second half of of the line. **sic ferebant:** *were tending that
way*; **fero** is often used in that sense with a word like **sic** replacing a
direct object. **fata** is poetic plural.

3 Rejoicing in Troy

Thinking they had left, the Trojans joyfully poured out of the city. Why had the Greeks left the horse? There was a division of opinion on what to do with it.

> nos abiisse rati et vento petiisse Mycenas.
> 15 ergo omnis longo solvit se Teucria luctu.
> panduntur portae; iuvat ire et Dorica castra
> desertosque videre locos litusque relictum.
> "hic Dolopum manus, hic saevus tendebat Achilles.
> classibus hic locus. hic acie certare solebant."
> 20 pars stupet innuptae donum exitiale Minervae
> et molem mirantur equi. primusque Thymoetes
> duci intra muros hortatur et arce locari,
> sive dolo seu iam Troiae sic fata ferebant.

24 **quorum melior sententia menti:** Supply *those* as the antecedent of the relative clause and *erat* as its verb: literally *those to whose minds was a better opinion*, i.e. *those whose judgement was sounder.*

25 **pelago:** dative with **praecipitare:** literally *to throw it to the sea*, like throwing food to an animal. Translate *into the sea.* **Danaum insidias suspectaque dona:** Much more than *the horse*, since this fine-sounding expression captures the conflicting emotions which the various Trojans felt about the horse. **Danaum:** See line 7.

26 Capys and those who supported him suggested three ways of dealing with the horse because they suspected treachery: (a) throw it into the sea, (b) burn it, (c) examine its hollow interior carefully. This explains the use of **-que**, since it would be difficult and silly to try to burn it after throwing it into the sea. Translate **-que** as *or.* **subiectis flammis:** Not ablative absolute, but Ablative of Instrument, i.e. what they used to burn it (LN # 12).

28 **studia in contraria:** This refers to the arguments among the crowd in general, some taking the side of Capys, others supporting the opposing view of Thymoetes. Translate *wavering* (**incertum**) *between the conflicting proposals.*

29 **ibi:** *at that moment.* **magna comitante caterva:** ablative absolute.

30 **Laocoon:** the son of Priam and priest of Apollo. **ardens:** a colourful word which expresses his excitement and the strength of his feelings.

31 **et procul:** Although there is no verb, the direct speech taken together with **procul** would suggest a word like *shouted*. In his excitement he does not wait until he reaches the scene before shouting his advice. **quae tanta insania:** *what utter madness (is this)?*

32 **avectos:** Supply **esse.**

33 **Danaum:** Take with **dona.** **notus:** Supply **est.** He implies that they should know better than to trust Ulysses because he was so renowned for his cunning.

34 **hoc ligno:** For the omission of the preposition see LN # 1. Note the contempt in *this bit of wood.* **Achivi:** *Achaeans*; yet another name used by Virgil for *Greeks* (see page 122).

35 **in nostros muros:** **in** used with the accusative to mean *against.* Translate *to threaten our walls.*

36 **error:** Something to take them off the track, i.e. a *trick* or *deception.* **ne credite:** a poetic form of **nolite credere.**

37 **et dona ferentes:** *even when they are bringing gifts.* This line has become proverbial: never trust an enemy, no matter how friendly he appears to be.

38 **sic fatus:** In the original tradition, this sort of poem (an epic) would have been sung by a minstrel, not read from a book. This type of

at Capys, et quorum melior sententia menti,
25   aut pelago Danaum insidias suspectaque dona
praecipitare iubent, subiectisque urere flammis;
aut terebrare cavas uteri et temptare latebras.
scinditur incertum studia in contraria vulgus.

4 Laocoon's warning

Laocoon was in no doubt: "The Greeks can't be trusted.
Destroy the horse!"

primus ibi ante omnes, magna comitante caterva,
30   Laocoon ardens summa decurrit ab arce;
et procul "o miseri, quae tanta insania, cives?
creditis avectos hostes?   aut ulla putatis
dona carere dolis Danaum?   sic notus Ulixes?
aut hoc inclusi ligno occultantur Achivi,
35   aut haec in nostros fabricata est machina muros
aut aliquis latet error.   equo ne credite, Teucri!
quidquid id est, timeo Danaos et dona ferentes."
sic fatus validis ingentem viribus hastam
contorsit.   stetit illa tremens, uteroque recusso
40   insonuere cavae gemitumque dedere cavernae.

---

phrase was used to tell the audience that the direct speech had ended
and the narrative was recommencing. (Compare **haec ubi dicta,
dixerat, sic ait, talia voce refert, his dictis** and **sic memorat.**) (See
LN # 39.)

39 The powerful caesura in the second foot and the rhythm of **stetit illa
tremens** conveys by sound the shuddering of the spear as it struck the
horse. The rest of the line and line 40 then depict the booming echo
within the body.   **utero recusso:** literally *the womb having been
struck back (by the spear)* thus producing an echo. Translate *from the
reverberations of the belly*.

40 **insonuere = insonuerunt. cavae** is used predicatively – *sounded
hollow*. (LN # 36)

line

41 **manus post terga revinctum: manus** is an Accusative of Respect (LN # 9): the young man was tied up *as far as his hands were concerned.* Translate *with his hands tied behind his back.*

43 **visendi studio:** literally *from an eagerness of seeing,* i.e. *in their eagerness to get a glimpse of him.* **iuventus** means little more than *the people* here. (See AIC 299.)

44 **circumfusa:** literally *having been poured round.* With **ruit** it means *poured round.* **certant:** The change from the singular verb (**ruit**) is quite natural. **capto:** perfect participle used as a noun – *the prisoner.*

45 **accipe:** *learn* or *hear.* **crimine ab uno:** *from the treachery of one of them.*

46 **omnes:** Supply **Danaos.** Another unfinished line. (See AIC 185.)

47 **ut:** with indicative = *as* or *when.* **conspectu in medio:** literally *in the middle of our sight,* i.e. *in our midst where we could all see him.*

48 **circumspexit:** The spondee in the fifth foot is unusual. Its 'heavy' effect helps convey his sense of hopelessness.

49 **quae tellus:** Supply **me accipere potest. quae** is an interrogative adjective.

50 **misero mihi:** literally *for miserable me,* i.e. *for me in my misery.* **denique:** *in short.* **denique** sums up his whole hopeless position.

51 **locus:** Supply **est. super:** used adverbially, *besides,* i.e. besides his own countrymen.

52 **Dardanidae:** *Trojans.* Dardanus was the mythical ancestor of the Trojans; the ending **-ides** means *the son of* (cf. Scottish *Mac* and Irish *O* as in MacDonald and O'Donnell). See page 122 for a list of the various names used by Virgil for the Trojans.

55 **ficto pectore:** *with false heart, with lying intent.*

5 A prisoner is brought in

At that moment, a Greek prisoner was brought in and caused a stir among the Trojans.

> ecce!   manus iuvenem interea post terga revinctum
> pastores magno ad regem clamore trahebant.
> undique visendi studio Troiana iuventus
> circumfusa ruit, certantque inludere capto.
> 45 accipe nunc Danaum insidias, et crimine ab uno
> disce omnes!
> namque ut conspectu in medio turbatus inermis
> constitit, atque oculis Phrygia agmina circumspexit:
> "heu!   quae nunc tellus," inquit "quae me aequora possu
> 50 accipere?   aut quid iam misero mihi denique restat,
> cui neque apud Danaos usquam locus, et super ipsi
> Dardanidae infensi poenas cum sanguine poscunt?"
> tum vero ardemus scitari et quaerere causas
> ignari scelerum tantorum artisque Pelasgae.
> 55 prosequitur pavitans, et ficto pectore fatur.

line

56 **his lacrimis:** literally *we gave his life to these tears*, i.e. (*persuaded*) *by these tears, we granted him his life.*

57 **viro:** What is called an ethic dative, which has the same force as a possessive genitive here: *the man's handcuffs.*

58 **vincla:** a shortened form of **vincula**, useful in poetry.
amicis: *friendly.*

59 **hinc iam:** hinc is used here in a temporal sense – *from this moment on.* **obliviscere** is imperative. **amissos:** *lost, whom you have lost*, since they were no longer to be regarded as his countrymen.

60 **noster eris:** *you will be one of us.* **mihi roganti:** literally *to me asking*, i.e. *in answer to my questions.* **vera** is used predicatively: *explain these things true*, i.e. *truthfully.* (LN # 36)

61 **quo:** *for what purpose?* **molem:** See line 21. **immanis:** Although this adjective agrees with **equi**, in an English translation it would more naturally be taken with **molem** (Transferred Epithet: LN # 14). **statuere = statuerunt.** **auctor:** literally *author*, i.e. (*who*) *thought of it?*

62 **quae religio: religio** does not mean *religion* but *religious observance*, i.e. *what holy offering is it?*

63 **dixerat:** For this convention compare line 38. *He finished speaking.* (LN # 39). **dolis instructus:** *well trained in treachery.*

64 **coepti fiducia belli:** *the confidence with which they began the war.*

65 **Palladis:** See line 8. **auxiliis:** poetic plural. The ablative shows what their confidence depended on. **stetit:** *rested, had its foundation.* **stare** is a strong word which suggests something firmly founded. **ex quo:** *from the moment when.*

66 **Tydides:** Diomede, the son of Tydeus. (Cf. line 52.)
sed enim: *however*; Virgil often has it late in the sentence.
scelerum inventor Ulixes: Note again Ulysses' reputation for cunning. Compare line 33.

67 **Palladium:** According to legend, Troy could not be captured as long as the statue of Pallas Athene was in its citadel. **summae arcis:** *the upper part of the citadel*; there would be a succession of defence lines, culminating at the highest part of the citadel where the Palladium was kept.

68 **corripuere:** See line 61.

69 **ausi:** Supply **sunt.** **contingere:** *to touch*, i.e. *to defile*; compare the English word *contagion.* **virgineas vittas:** Pallas was an unwed goddess, and the adjective suggests the purity of the virgin.

6 Sinon's story

The Trojans, feeling in a generous mood, urged Sinon to tell his story. He said he was a Greek who had fled from the Greeks to save his life. In the past he had angered Ulysses, and now Ulysses was bent on revenge. The Greeks had long wanted to abandon the siege of Troy but had been prevented by storms from going home. On consulting the oracle of Apollo they had been told that only a human sacrifice could appease the winds and secure them a safe return home. At Ulysses' bidding, the priest had named Sinon as the victim, but on the day of the sacrifice he had escaped and had decided to throw himself on the mercy of the Trojans.

7 Sinon set free

We were deceived by the story. Priam set him free and asked him to explain the significance of the horse.

> his lacrimis vitam damus et miserescimus ultro.
> ipse viro primus manicas atque arta levari
> vincla iubet Priamus, dictisque ita fatur amicis:
> "quisquis es, amissos hinc iam obliviscere Graios!
> 60 noster eris; mihique haec edissere vera roganti!
> quo molem hanc immanis equi statuere?   quis auctor?
> quidve petunt?   quae religio?   aut quae machina belli?"

8 Sinon's story

According to Sinon, Pallas Athene had turned against the Greeks from the moment Diomede and Ulysses had violated her temple and carried off her statue.

> dixerat.   ille dolis instructus et arte Pelasga
> "omnis spes Danaum et coepti fiducia belli
> 65 Palladis auxiliis semper stetit.   impius ex quo
> Tydides sed enim scelerumque inventor Ulixes
> Palladium, caesis summae custodibus arcis,
> corripuere sacram effigiem, manibusque cruentis
> virgineas ausi divae contingere vittas;

70 **ex illo:** This takes up the **ex quo** in line 65: *from that moment on* (cf. **hinc** in line 59). **fluere ac retro sublapsa referri: fluere** and **referri** are historic infinitives which can be translated like indicatives (*began*) *to ebb and slip back slowly*. It is the metaphor of the sea gradually going out, and the historic infinitive conveys the idea of a continual process rather than a distinct action (LN # 23).

71 **fractae:** Supply **sunt**; the perfect indicative marks the sudden turning point in their fortunes. (Contrast the historic infinitive in the previous line.) (Supply **est** with **aversa**.) **aversa deae mens:** literally *the goddess's mind was turned away from them*, i.e. *the support of the goddess was lost*. The goddess is, of course, Pallas Athene.

72 **nec dubiis monstris:** Two negatives make a very strong positive: *not doubtful* = *clear* or *definite*. (Compare **non ignara** in AIC 246.) The noun **monstrum** is related to the verb **monstrare**, *to show*: it was the means whereby the gods showed mortals what they wished – *omens* or *portents*. **ea signa:** literally *those signs*, i.e. *signs of that* (the changes referred to in lines 70–71). **Tritonia** is yet another name for Pallas Athene and Minerva: she was said to have been born at Lake Triton in North Africa.

73 **temptanda:** Supply **esse**. By scanning the line, we see that it agrees with **aequora** and that **fuga** is ablative. The accusative and infinitive depends on **canit:** literally *that the sea must be tried by means of flight*, i.e. *they should try to escape across the sea*. **canit:** *interpreted the omens by declaring*. This verb is used since the priest would chant his prophecies. **aequora:** poetic plural.

74 **nec posse . . . Pergama:** This accusative and infinitive continues what Calchas said. **Pergama** was the inner citadel of Troy. **Pergama** is neuter plural.

75 **omina ni repetant Argis:** literally *unless they re-sought propitious signs from Argos*, i.e. unless they went back to Argos and again sought the blessing of the gods. If something unlucky happened during an enterprise, the only way to win back divine support was to go back to the start and offer up a fresh sacrifice. **Argis** is ablative. Argos was the capital city of the Danai, and therefore it means little more than *Greece* here. **numen** refers to the statue of Pallas which had been carried off to Greece (line 67) and which symbolised 'the goodwill and favourable power of the goddess'.

76 **quod:** *which* referring to **numen**. **pelago:** literally *by* (*means of*) *the sea*, i.e. *over the sea*. **avexere:** See line 61. **curvis carinis:** See line 12 for this use of **carina** (LN # 32). Why is the adjective **curvus** used? For the omission of the preposition see LN # 1.

77 **hanc** agrees with **effigiem**, i.e. the wooden horse. **pro numine laeso:** *to make amends for the wrong done to the goddess*. (Cf. AIC 11 for this idiom where the emphasis in Latin is on the participle, but

70   ex illo fluere ac retro sublapsa referri
      spes Danaum, fractae vires, aversa deae mens.
      nec dubiis ea signa dedit Tritonia monstris.

9 A peace-offering to Pallas

The Greeks decided that the only solution was to go back
to Greece and start the expedition again. The horse was a
peace-offering to the goddess, and it had been made too
large for the Trojans to get it into the city. If they did, the
power of the goddess would pass to the Trojans, and one
day they would destroy Greece.

      "extemplo temptanda fuga canit aequora Calchas;
      nec posse Argolicis exscindi Pergama telis,
75   omina ni repetant Argis numenque reducant,
      quod pelago et curvis secum avexere carinis.
      hanc pro Palladio moniti, pro numine laeso
      effigiem statuere, nefas quae triste piaret.
      hanc tamen immensam Calchas attollere molem
80   roboribus textis, caeloque educere iussit,
      ne recipi portis aut duci in moenia possit.

English prefers to use a noun.)   **moniti:** literally *having been
advised* (by Calchas), i.e. *on his advice.*

78 **statuere:** See line 61.   **quae piaret** is a purpose clause. The *cursed
crime* was, of course, the carrying off of the Palladium to Greece.

79 **hanc immensam molem:** again refers to the horse.   **tamen** therefore
does not draw a contrast with lines 77–78; it rather brings in the extra
point: make it really big – **immensam**, which is used predicatively
here. (LN # 36)

80 **roboribus textis:** literally *with woven oak planks*, i.e. *with interwoven
planks of oak.* This is an Ablative of Instrument, showing what they
used (LN # 12).   **caelo:** dative, used poetically for **in caelum**.
iussit: The subject is **Calchas** (line 79), and the object is **Troianos**
(understood).

81 **ne ... possit:** a negative purpose clause.   **portis:** literally *(re-
ceived) by the gates*, i.e. *(taken in) through the gates.*

82 **violasset:** shortened form of **violavisset**. The pluperfect subjunctive is brought about by the indirect speech: (*he said that*) *if . . . had violated, . . . would . . . .* Translate *violated*. **manus** is singular because it would require only one hand to do the damage. **Minervae:** Although genitive, this is best translated as *offering* **to** *Minerva* (cf. line 20). (LN # 6)

83 **quod omen:** linking relative: *that terrible fate.*   **in ipsum:** refers to Calchas.

84 **convertant:** a wish – *may* (*the gods*) *turn*.   **futurum:** Supply **esse**. The accusative and infinitive continues Calchas' prediction. Translate *would befall*.   **Phrygibus:** another name for the Trojans. See page 122.

85 **ascendisset:** Compare **violasset** (line 82) for explanation of the use of the pluperfect subjunctive. Literally *but if it had ascended*, i.e. *if it were brought up*.   **manibus:** In contrast with line 82, many hands would be required to pull it into the city.

86 **ultro:** This word usually suggests something over and above what you might expect, Troy wouldn't be content simply with being saved but would carry the offensive to Greece. Translate *unprovoked*. **Asiam venturam (esse):** Compare line 84.   **Pelopea ad moenia:** *to the cities of Greece* (cf. line 14). Pelops had founded the royal family at Mycenae. The Peloponnese is named after him.

87 **ea fata manere:** The change of tense from **venturam** is interesting; it suggests that *that fate* (*of being attacked by Troy*) **is actually** *awaiting*.   **nostros:** Remember it is a Greek who is speaking.

88 **talibus insidiis:** For this use of **talis** to indicate the end of the direct speech cf. line 38. Translate *thanks to this sort of trickery*. (LN # 39)

89 **credita res:** Supply **est** – *the story was believed*.   **capti:** Supply **sumus** – *we were taken in*.   **coactis:** They were *forced* because they did not come naturally. He was play-acting.

90 **quos:** The antecedent is 'we' contained in **capti**.   **Larissaeus:** Achilles' kingdom was in Larissa, part of Thessaly.

91 **non . . . non . . . :** These words continue **nec . . . nec . . .**, but even more powerfully.   **domuere:** See line 61.

92 **hic:** *At this point.*   **aliud maius:** literally *another greater thing*, i.e. *another omen greater and . . .*   **multo:** Take with **magis**. **miseris:** (*to us*) *poor wretched beings*.

94 **ductus sorte:** *drawn* (i.e. *chosen*) *by lot*. Neptune was one of the gods who protected Troy because he had helped to build its walls (cf. AIC 60 ff).

95 **aras:** poetic plural.

nam si vestra manus violasset dona Minervae,
tum magnum exitium (quod di prius omen in ipsum
convertant!) Priami imperio Phrygibusque futurum.
85 sin manibus vestris vestram ascendisset in urbem,
ultro Asiam magno Pelopea ad moenia bello
venturam, et nostros ea fata manere nepotes."
talibus insidiis periurique arte Sinonis
credita res, captique dolis lacrimisque coactis,
90 quos neque Tydides nec Larissaeus Achilles,
non anni domuere decem, non mille carinae.

Minerva or Pallas Athene

10 A terrible fate

At that moment, a terrible omen filled our hearts with fear.
While Laocoon was making sacrifice on the shore, two
monstrous snakes, with blood-red crests, flashing eyes and
hissing tongues, suddenly appeared in the sea and swam
straight towards Laocoon and his sons.

hic aliud maius miseris multoque tremendum
obicitur magis, atque improvida pectora turbat.
Laocoon, ductus Neptuno sorte sacerdos,
95 sollemnes taurum ingentem mactabat ad aras.

96 **gemini:** Agrees with **angues** (line 97). **per alta:** *across the sea.* Note how in lines 96–98 Virgil adds to the scene little by little. It is important therefore to translate the words in this dramatic order.

97 **referens:** *as I tell the tale.*

98 **incumbunt pelago:** *breasted the sea.*

99 **fit sonitus:** The rhythm of the words conveys the shock the Trojans felt when the sound first struck them, and the sound-effects are continued in **spumante salo**, so that the four uses of 's' convey the splashing of the water around the snakes. (Alliteration: LN # 33). **tenebant:** *they were reaching.*

100 A vivid description, conveyed by the words and the metre. The 's' sounds suggest the hissing of their flickering tongues, while the 'l' sounds suggest their slimy bodies gliding through the water.

101 **agmine certo: agmen** normally describes the column of an army on the march. Here, the long bodies of the snakes create the same impression. Translate *with unswerving course.*

102 **Laocoonta:** Accusative case (Greek accusative: LN # 4); five syllables: **La-o-co-on-ta**.

104 **morsu depascitur:** literally *devoured with a bite*, i.e. they plunged their fangs into the limbs and began to eat them.

105 **post** is used adverbially – *then.* **ipsum auxilio subeuntem: ipsum** refers to Laocoon; **auxilio** is a predicative dative denoting purpose – *as he came to their aid.*

107 **medium amplexi:** Supply **eum** with **medium** – *they wound themselves round his waist.*
collo squamea circum terga dati: This is a very complex piece of Latin. Firstly, in **circum . . . dati**, we have an example of Tmesis, the splitting of a word into two parts (cf. AIC 84 and LN # 28). The rest of the construction is most easily understood by looking at what the Latin would have been if it had been expressed actively: **terga collo circumdederunt**, *they wound their backs round his neck* (**collo** is dative). The verb **circumdo** also appears in the passive with a reflexive meaning – *to wind oneself round.* The Greek language had a special part of the verb to express this, namely, the Middle Voice (neither Active nor Passive), which could also take a direct object as well as expressing the reflexive idea (LN # 20). Virgil imitates that Greek construction here, even though he has to use the Latin Passive Voice instead of the Greek Middle Voice. In spite of all this, the meaning of the Latin is clear: *they twined their scaly backs around his neck and . . . .*

108 **superant:** *they towered over him.* The basic idea of **superare** is *to be above*, hence its extension to the idea of superiority and defeating.

ecce autem gemini a Tenedo tranquilla per alta
(horresco referens) immensis orbibus angues
incumbunt pelago, pariterque ad litora tendunt.
fit sonitus, spumante salo. iamque arva tenebant.
100 sibila lambebant linguis vibrantibus ora.
diffugimus visu exsangues. illi agmine certo
Laocoonta petunt. et primum parva duorum
corpora natorum serpens amplexus uterque
implicat, et miseros morsu depascitur artus.
105 post ipsum auxilio subeuntem et tela ferentem
corripiunt spirisque ligant ingentibus. et iam
bis medium amplexi, bis collo squamea circum
terga dati, superant capite et cervicibus altis.

Laocoon and his two sons being devoured by serpents.

109 **ille:** *he.* The abrupt use of the pronoun shifts attention from the snakes to Laocoon's desperate attempts to free himself from their coils.

110 **ad sidera:** It is daytime, but the poet is allowed this piece of poetic licence; translate *to the heavens.*

111 **qualis mugitus:** Supply **est** – *it was just like the bellowing.* Note how the 'u' sounds (5 in two lines) suggest bellowing. The simile is introduced, as frequently, by **qualis.** (Cf. AIC 146 and LN # 26.)

112 **incertam securim:** *a badly aimed blow of the axe.* To perform the sacrifice properly, the priest should deal a crisp, clean blow to the animal. The sacrifice is also spoiled by the horror of the doomed animal struggling to escape.

113 **at:** Attention is shifted back to the snakes. **lapsu effugiunt:** literally *they escaped with gliding.* Translate *they glided away and escaped* or *gliding away, they escaped.* **delubra ad summa:** Remember that Pallas Athene's temple was on the citadel. **delubra** is poetic plural.

114 **Tritonidis:** Tritonis was yet another name for Pallas Athene (cf. line 72).

115 **pedibus deae:** This refers to the statue of the goddess which stood in the temple. **teguntur:** *concealed themselves* – another use of the passive to express a reflexive idea (LN # 20).

116 **cunctis:** dative case – literally *as far as all of us were concerned.* It is most neatly translated as *of all of us.*

117 **scelus expendisse:** *had paid for his crime.* **expendisse Laocoonta** is an accusative and infinitive depending on **ferunt** (*they said*). **merentem:** literally *deserving*; English would say *deservedly.*

118 **qui laeserit:** Causal subjunctive giving the reason they gave for their judgement: *in that he had violated.* **sacrum robur:** the material standing for *the horse* which was made from the oak; and it is described as *sacred* since it had been dedicated to Pallas Athene by the Greeks.

119 **tergo:** probably *body*, rather than *back.*

120 **ducendum simulacrum:** Supply **esse** – an accusative and infinitive depending on **conclamant** – *that the wooden horse should be brought.* **sedes:** poetic plural – *the temple.*

121 An unfinished line. (See AIC 185.)

122 **dividimus muros:** The horse was too big to go through the gateway. The Trojans therefore had to break through the part of the wall above the gates, thus weakening their defences.
moenia: *fortifications* rather than *walls.*

123 **accingunt:** Supply **se.**

ille simul manibus tendit divellere nodos.

110 clamores simul horrendos ad sidera tollit.
qualis mugitus, fugit cum saucius aram
taurus et incertam excussit cervice securim.
at gemini lapsu delubra ad summa dracones
effugiunt, saevaeque petunt Tritonidis arcem,

115 sub pedibusque deae clipeique sub orbe teguntur.

11 The horse is taken into the city

Immediately there were shouts that Laocoon had deserved his fate. The Trojans tore down the wall and, amidst great rejoicing, hauled the horse into the city.

tum vero tremefacta novus per pectora cunctis
insinuat pavor; et scelus expendisse merentem
Laocoonta ferunt, sacrum qui cuspide robur
laeserit, et tergo sceleratam intorserit hastam.

120 ducendum ad sedes simulacrum, orandaque divae
numina conclamant.
dividimus muros et moenia pandimus urbis.
accingunt omnes operi, pedibusque rotarum
subiciunt lapsus, et stuppea vincula collo

125 intendunt.   scandit fatalis machina muros,
feta armis: pueri circum innuptaeque puellae
sacra canunt, funemque manu contingere gaudent.

---

124 **rotarum lapsus:** literally *the glidings of wheels*, i.e. *wheels* (or *rollers*) *to help it glide along.*

125 **intendunt:** This means more than *tied*. It suggests the tautness of the rope ready for the pulling.   **scandit:** A picturesque touch – a new way of *scaling walls.*

126 **feta armis:** Note the dramatic effect of delaying these words to the end of the sentence.   **circum** is an adverb.

127 **sacra canunt:** *sang hymns.*   **contingere gaudent:** Compare the hero-worship so common today.

128 **illa** refers to the **machina.** **minans:** *looking menacingly down upon.*

129 A passionate outburst by Aeneas as his emotions overwhelm him in the midst of telling his story. **divom = divorum** (LN # 5). **incluta bello:** *famed in war.*

131 **substitit:** The abrupt pause at the end of the first foot effectively illustrates the sticking of the horse in the gateway. **dedere:** See line 61.

132 **instamus tamen:** The sound conveys their blind determination. **immemores:** They had forgotten that it was unlucky to stumble when crossing a threshold (which explains why Roman brides were carried across). *Heedless* refers to this warning and to the fact that they ignored the rumbling from within the horse.

133 **sacrata arce:** See LN # 1 for omission of the preposition.

134 **tunc etiam:** *then again*: There had been other occasions when Cassandra had warned the Trojans of impending disaster. The god Apollo had fallen in love with her in days gone by, but she had rejected his love. To punish her, Apollo had given her the gift of being able to prophesy the future but also decreed that no one would ever believe her. (See line 135.)

135 **ora:** poetic plural. **Teucris** is Dative of Agent, often used in poetry with passive verbs (LN # 7).

136 **deum = deorum** (LN # 5). **quibus . . . esset:** The antecedent of **quibus** is **nos.** The verb (**esset**) is Causal subjunctive explaining **miseri:** *we poor souls, for that was our last day.*

137 Scan the line to see whether the **-a** of **festa** is long or short.

illa subit, mediaeque minans inlabitur urbi.
o patria, o divom domus Ilium, et incluta bello
130 moenia Dardanidum! quater ipso in limine portae
substitit, atque utero sonitum quater arma dedere.
instamus tamen immemores caecique furore,
et monstrum infelix sacrata sistimus arce.
tunc etiam fatis aperit Cassandra futuris
135 ora, dei iussu non umquam credita Teucris.
nos delubra deum miseri, quibus ultimus esset
ille dies, festa velamus fronde per urbem.

line

138 **vertitur:** The ancients believed that the sky was a huge sphere which encircled the earth. One half of it was black, the other bright. As it revolved, the bright half brought daylight, the dark half darkness. **Oceano:** *from the sea.* The abrupt sound of the single syllable word **nox** at the end of the line conveys the suddenness with which darkness falls in the Mediterranean.

140 **Myrmidonum:** The Myrmidons were the warriors of Achilles; here, the term is used for the Greeks in general. (Cf. lines 34 and 75.) **fusi:** They had been eating and drinking and so they were *sprawling* anyhow and anywhere.

143 A beautiful line depicting the still silence as they crept up on the unsuspecting Trojans. Even the moon seemed to be conspiring against the Trojans and favouring the Greeks.

145 **laxat** is used in two senses here: he *undid* the bars locking the opening into the horse, and *released* the soldiers inside. (Zeugma: LN # 29.) Note also that the time sequence of events (**Danaos et claustra laxat**) is reversed, an example of the figure of speech called Hysteron Proteron. (See LN # 35.) **illos:** *them* (the Greeks inside the horse). **ad auras:** *to the (open) air.*

148 **Pelides Neoptolemus:** Neoptolemus was the son of Achilles, who was himself the son of Peleus. **Pelides** here means *descendant of Peleus* (cf. line 52). **primus:** For once, Virgil seems to use an inappropriate adjective. It cannot mean that Machaon came out first (**duces** in line 147 means that); nor can it mean that Machaon was a distinguished leader or warrior. He was actually a physician rather than a warrior. Possibly it means he was *unrivalled* (in his own sphere, as a doctor).

149 **doli fabricator:** The *trick* was, of course, the wooden horse itself.

152 **accipiunt:** Note the change of subject, although it is not a difficult jump in one's thinking: the Greeks had been responsible for killing the guards. **agmina conscia** are those inside the city and those attacking from outside. They are said to be **conscia** since they were both party to the plot.

12 The Greeks return

At night, when the Trojans were asleep and weary from their celebrations, the Greeks sailed back.

vertitur interea caelum, et ruit Oceano nox,
involvens umbra magna terramque polumque
140 Myrmidonumque dolos.   fusi per moenia Teucri
conticuere.   sopor fessos complectitur artus.
et iam Argiva phalanx instructis navibus ibat
a Tenedo tacitae per amica silentia lunae.

13 Sinon opens up the horse

Seizing his chance, Sinon released the men from the horse. They slew the guards at the gates and joined forces with their friends from the ships.

inclusos utero Danaos et pinea furtim
145 laxat claustra Sinon.   illos patefactus ad auras
reddit equus; laetique cavo se robore promunt
Thessandrus Sthenelusque duces, et dirus Ulixes,
Pelidesque Neoptolemus, primusque Machaon,
et Menelaus, et ipse doli fabricator Epeos.
150 invadunt urbem somno vinoque sepultam.
caeduntur vigiles, portisque patentibus omnes
accipiunt socios, atque agmina conscia iungunt.

153 **quo:** *at which, when* (Ablative of *Time When*).   **aegris:** *weary, exhausted.*

154 **dono divom gratissima serpit:** A wealth of meaning is packed into these words. **gratissima serpit** describes the very pleasant sensation one experiences as one is dropping off to sleep; **gratissima** also contains the idea of *most welcome*, as a change from toil. Finally, sleep comes *as a gift from the gods*; it is one of the greatest blessings man has, since it can cure mental as well as physical pain.

156 **visus:** Supply **est**.

157 **qualis erat:** *what a sight he was.*

158 **exuvias indutus Achilli:** Compare line 107 for this use of a passive verb governing an accusative. The active form would be **exuvias induere**, *to put on the spoils*; in the passive **indutus** means *dressed*. In this construction (imitating a construction used in Greek), the two uses are brought together: *dressed in the spoils* (LN # 20).

Earlier in the siege, when Achilles refused to fight in battle because of a quarrel with Agamemnon, his friend Patroclus had gone out to face Hector dressed in Achilles' armour. This attempt to save his friend's reputation against a charge of cowardice cost Patroclus his own life. After slaying Patroclus, Hector returned in triumph to Troy wearing the captured armour. Later, in revenge, Achilles slew Hector and dragged his body round the walls of Troy behind his chariot. He later returned the body to Priam when the latter came to his camp to plead for its return.

159 **squalentem barbam:** direct object of **gerens** (line 160), which means little more than *having* in this context. With **vulnera**, *showing* is a better translation.

160 **circum** governs **muros**.   **plurima:** Take with **vulnera**. (See note on line 158.) In Latin, superlatives are frequently attracted into the relative clause (LN # 16).

161 **ultro:** *first*, i.e. without waiting for Hector to speak.
videbar: *I seemed*, i.e. *I dreamed.*

162 **voces:** *words.*

163 **lux:** *light* in the sense of someone who brings *glory*.
Teucrum = Teucrorum. (Cf. **Danaum** in line 7 and **deum** in line 136.)

164 **quae tantae tenuere morae?:** **morae** is poetic plural. With **tenuere** (for form see line 61) supply **te**. He means *what has kept you so long?*

165 **exspectate:** vocative case, attracted into the case of **Hector:** *you whom we have long awaited.*   **ut:** Take with **aspicimus** – *how (gladly) we behold you.*   **post funera:** Take with **defessi**.

14 A vision appears

While I slept, the ghost of Hector, who had been slain by Achilles, appeared to me in a dream and bade me save the gods of Troy by finding a new home for them in another land.

tempus erat quo prima quies mortalibus aegris
incipit, et dono divom gratissima serpit.
155   in somnis, ecce, ante oculos maestissimus Hector
visus adesse mihi, largoque effundere fletus.
hei mihi!   qualis erat!   quantum mutatus ab illo
Hectore, qui redit exuvias indutus Achilli!
squalentem barbam et concretos sanguine crines
160   vulneraque illa gerens quae circum plurima muros
accepit patrios.   ultro flens ipse videbar
compellare virum et maestas expromere voces:
"o lux Dardaniae, spes o fidissima Teucrum,
quae tantae tenuere morae?   quibus, Hector, ab oris
165   exspectate venis?   ut te post multa tuorum

167 **quae causa:** Aeneas actually knew what had happened to Hector, but the mind plays strange tricks in dreams.

169 **ille nihil:** Supply **respondet**, but the two words are more effective on their own.   **nec moratur:** literally *and did not delay me*, i.e. did not waste time on my silly questions. Translate *and paid no heed.*

171 **nate dea:** a stock way of addressing Aeneas: literally *born from a goddess*, i.e. *O son of the goddess.* Aeneas was the son of Venus.

172 **ruit:** *is crashing in ruins.* This verb is used of buildings being completely destroyed, as if the walls were rushing to reach the ground as fast as possible.

173 **datum:** Supply **est.** Priam and Troy can ask for no more from you. **si possent . . . defensa fuissent:** an unreal condition: *if it could have been, . . . it would have been defended.*   **dextra:** *by a right hand*, i.e. by brave deeds.

174 **etiam hac:** Supply **dextra**; *even by this right hand (of mine).*

175 **sacra suosque Penates:** The **sacra** were all the sacred objects and emblems used to carry out the religious rites for the city. They would include the Penates, the family gods which looked after the city. Therefore translate **-que** as *including.* (LN # 37)

176 **hos cape comites: comites** is used predicatively – *take these as companions.* (LN # 36)

178 **ascensu supero:** See line 108 for the basic meaning of **supero.** A poetic way of saying *I climbed on to.*

179 **veluti cum:** *as when.* (**veluti** like **qualis** introduces a simile. See line 111.) (LN # 26)

180 **rapidus:** *swift*, i.e. sweeping everything with it. The word is derived from the same root as **rapere** (cf. AIC 29).

181 **sata laeta:** Poets often refer to crops as *joyful.* Several ideas are contained in the word **laetus:** healthy, plentiful, a pleasure to look at, heads erect and even dancing, as Wordsworth said of the daffodils.   **boum labores:** literally *the labours of the oxen*, i.e. *the fields ploughed by the oxen.* This is another use of the explanatory **-que** (cf. line 175), so that the translation might become *the joyful crops in the fields ploughed by the oxen.* (LN # 37)

182 **praecipites** is used predicatively (see line 176). (LN # 36)
inscius agrees with **pastor**, who is still somewhat bemused and doesn't fully understand what is happening.
alto agrees with **vertice.** Note that Virgil does not finish off the simile. His audience is left to draw the connection between the shepherd and Aeneas.

184 **virum = virorum** (cf. line 163). **-que . . . -que:** *both . . . and . . .*

funera, post varios hominumque urbisque labores
defessi aspicimus! quae causa indigna serenos
foedavit vultus? aut cur haec vulnera cerno?"
ille nihil. nec me quaerentem vana moratur,
170 sed graviter gemitus imo de pectore ducens
"heu! fuge, nate dea! teque his" ait "eripe flammis!
hostis habet muros. ruit alto a culmine Troia.
sat patriae Priamoque datum. si Pergama dextra
defendi possent, etiam hac defensa fuissent.
175 sacra suosque tibi commendat Troia Penates.
hos cape fatorum comites! his moenia quaere!"

15 Aeneas awakes

When I woke, I climbed to the roof of my house and
listened to the noise of battle. My first reaction was to fight
to the death.

excutior somno, et summi fastigia tecti
ascensu supero, atque arrectis auribus adsto.
in segetem veluti cum flamma furentibus Austris
180 incidit, aut rapidus montano flumine torrens
sternit agros, sternit sata laeta boumque labores,
praecipitesque trahit silvas, stupet inscius alto
accipiens sonitum saxi de vertice pastor.
exoritur clamorque virum clangorque tubarum.
185 arma amens capio; nec sat rationis in armis.

---

185 **nec sat rationis:** Supply **est mihi** = *I had*; **rationis** is partitive genitive. The literal meaning is *I had not enough of a plan*, i.e. *I had
no clear idea of how I planned (to fight)*.

186 **bello:** dative of purpose – *for battle* or *to fight*. (LN # 8)

187 **ardent animi: animi** is poetic plural: *my heart longed*, i.e. *I had a strong desire.*

188 **pulchrum mori succurrit in armis:** literally *to die in arms struck (me) as a beautiful thing*, the infinitive **mori** being the subject of **succurrit**. Translate *The thought occurred to me that it was a glorious thing to die fighting.*

189 **Achivom:** genitive plural. (LN # 5)

191 **sacra:** See line 175. **manu:** *in his hand.* **victos deos:** These were the small statues of the gods. They are said to be **victos** because it is already obvious that Troy is about to fall.

192 **trahit:** The meaning *dragged* is appropriate only for **nepotem;** with **sacra** and **deos** *carried* would be a better verb. (Zeugma: LN # 29.) **cursu tendit:** Compare line 178 for this sort of poetic expression; it means *he was running.* **ad limina:** *to my door.*

193 **quo loco:** *where?* Supply **est. res summa:** *the main fighting.*

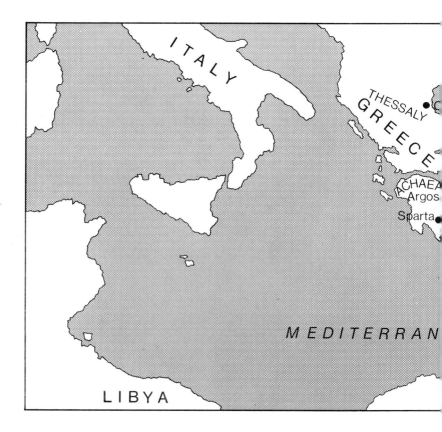

sed glomerare manum bello et concurrere in arcem
cum sociis ardent animi. furor iraque mentem
praecipitant; pulchrumque mori succurrit in armis.

16 He meets Panthus

Panthus shouted to me that all was lost, but the frenzy of
battle still urged me on.

ecce autem telis Panthus elapsus Achivom,
190   Panthus Othryades, arcis Phoebique sacerdos,
sacra manu victosque deos parvumque nepotem
ipse trahit, cursuque amens ad limina tendit.
"quo res summa loco, Panthu?   quam prendimus arcem?"

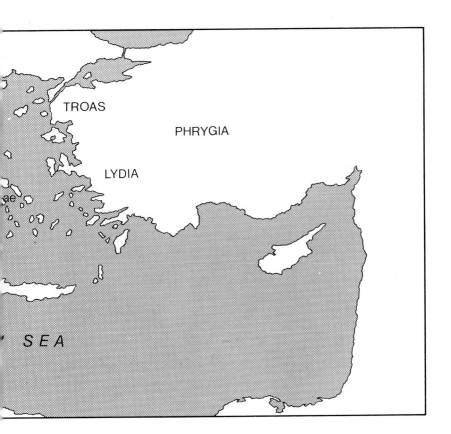

TROAS

PHRYGIA

LYDIA

ae

SEA

194 **talia:** *as follows.* See line 38 for the poetic convention which indicates the start and finish of direct speech (LN # 39).
ineluctabile: They could fight as much as they liked: the Fates had decided that Troy should fall.

196 **fuimus:** The perfect tense indicates a completed action – *we have been (and are no more),* i.e. we are done for. (Cf. the slang *'a has-been'.)* **Ilium:** another name for Troy, called after a former king. (From this word we get *Iliad,* the title of Homer's great epic.)

198 **arduus:** *towering high.* Note the emphatic position at the start of the sentence.

199 **victor:** He has achieved what he set out to do: *triumphantly.*
incendia miscet: The verb **miscere** (literally *to mix,* or *stir up*) is used to describe the creation of confusion. (See AIC 60 and 100.) We might say *is spreading fire and confusion.*

200 **talibus:** Compare line 194, although on this occasion the word refers to what has gone before. **numine divom:** *by the will of the gods.*

201 **quo:** *whither, where.* **Erinys** was the Fury who symbolised the slaughter and bloodshed of battle: *the grim (unsmiling) Fury.*

202 **aethera** is a Greek accusative. (Cf. line 102) (LN # 4)

203 **socios** is used predicatively – *as allies* (LN # 36).

204 **oblati per lunam:** The compound **ob-fero (offero)** means literally *I bring in the way of.* Rhipeus and Epytus were *brought into my path through the moon (light).* Translate *looming up before me in the moonlight.*

205 **adglomerant:** Supply **se.**

206 **illis diebus:** *recently.*

208 **gener:** *as a (future) son-in-law.*

209 **haud dubiam:** *certain* (cf. line 72).
mediaeque tenemus urbis iter: literally *and held our route of* (i.e. *to*) *the middle of the city,* i.e. *we made straight for the centre of the city.*

210 Scan the line to find out whether the final **-a** is long or short in **atra** and **cava.** Since **umbra** is the last word in the line, the **-a** may be long or short, but the rest of the sentence should help you decide.

211 **quis explicet?:** *who could describe (if he tried)?* The suppressed condition explains the use of the subjunctive. (Cf. **possit** in line 212.) **fando:** literally *by speaking,* i.e. *in words.* **funera fando:** Note the alliteration; also **lacrimis labores** in the next line (LN # 33).

213 **ruit:** See line 172.

214 **perque:** This is balanced by **perque** in line 215: *through (both)* . . . *and . . . .*

vix ea fatus eram, gemitu cum talia reddit:
195 "venit summa dies et ineluctabile tempus
Dardaniae. fuimus Troes. fuit Ilium et ingens
gloria Teucrorum. Danai dominantur in urbe.
arduus armatos mediis in moenibus adstans
fundit equus, victorque Sinon incendia miscet."
200 talibus Othryadae dictis et numine divom
in flammas et in arma feror, quo tristis Erinys,
quo fremitus vocat et sublatus ad aethera clamor.

17 The Trojans stage a recovery

I was joined by some friends and together we fought back
against the Greeks and killed many of them.

addunt se socios Rhipeus et maximus armis
Epytus, oblati per lunam, Hypanisque Dymasque,
205 et lateri adglomerant nostro, iuvenisque Coroebus
Mygdonides. illis ad Troiam forte diebus
venerat, insano Cassandrae incensus amore,
et gener auxilium Priamo Phrygibusque ferebat.
vadimus haud dubiam in mortem, mediaeque tenemus
210 urbis iter; nox atra cava circumvolat umbra.
quis cladem illius noctis, quis funera fando
explicet, aut possit lacrimis aequare labores?
urbs antiqua ruit multos dominata per annos.
plurima perque vias sternuntur inertia passim
215 corpora, perque domos et religiosa deorum
limina. nec soli poenas dant sanguine Teucri;

---

215 **religiosa deorum limina:** a poetic way of referring to temples.
216 The order of the words in this line is very effective.

line
217 quondam: *at times.* **etiam victis:** *even to the vanquished.* The dative has the force of a genitive, *the hearts of the vanquished.* Note the repetition of the **v-** sound in lines 217–218.

218 crudelis ubique luctus: Supply **est.**

219 pavor: The **-o-** is long. **plurima mortis imago:** *very many forms of death,* i.e. *death in countless shapes.*

220 se offert nobis: literally *offered himself to us,* i.e. *came up to meet us* thinking we were Greeks.

221 Androgeos: nominative singular (a Greek ending).
socia agmina: Supply **esse nostra** (accusative and infinitive depending on **credens**) and take **socia** predicatively (LN # 36).

222 inscius: *in his ignorance*; note the emphatic position which is given even greater impact by the strong pause after it.
ultro: Cf. line 161. **amicis** is an adjective.

223 tam sera: The idea of lateness is transferred to **segnities** which is really the cause of the lateness; translate *making you so late.*

224 rapiunt feruntque; literally *seize and carry off,* i.e. *are looting and plundering.*

225 vos itis?: *are you coming?*

226 dixit: See line 38 for this poetic convention (LN # 39).
neque fida satis: literally *not trustworthy enough*; the replies did not reassure him but made him suspicious.

227 sensit delapsus: This imitates a Greek construction – nominative of the participle, instead of accusative and infinitive, after certain verbs (seeing, noticing, etc.) where the same person is subject of both clauses. Translate *he realised that he had fallen.*

228 obstipuit: Again, the single word followed by the strong pause effectively conveys his sudden apprehension. (Cf. line 222.)
pedem cum voce: *his foot and his voice,* i.e. *both at the same time.*

229 veluti qui: For the use of **veluti** to introduce a simile compare line 179: *just like (someone) who* (LN # 26). **improvisum:** literally *unforeseen* (cf. AIC 218). Translate *unexpectedly* or *accidentally* – he hadn't expected to step on it. **aspris = asperis.** For **sentibus** without the preposition see LN # 1.

230 humi nitens: *as he puts his weight on the ground.*

231 attollentem iras: Supply **eum** as the object of **refugit:** *shrinks back from it as it raises its anger* (i.e. *rears its angry head*).
iras is poetic plural.

232 haud secus: Just as **veluti** introduces the simile, so **haud secus** marks the return to the main thread of the story. Compare the convention which shows the end of direct speech (see LN # 26 and lines 38, 63, 194 and 226); literally *not otherwise,* i.e. *just like that.* **treme-**

quondam etiam victis redit in praecordia virtus,
victoresque cadunt Danai. crudelis ubique
luctus, ubique pavor, et plurima mortis imago.

18 They find a victim

One of our first victims was Androgeos who mistook us for friends.

220   primus se, Danaum magna comitante caterva,
     Androgeos offert nobis, socia agmina credens
     inscius, atque ultro verbis compellat amicis:
     "festinate, viri! nam quae tam sera moratur
     segnities? alii rapiunt incensa feruntque
225   Pergama; vos celsis nunc primum a navibus itis?"
     dixit. et extemplo – neque enim responsa dabantur
     fida satis – sensit medios delapsus in hostes.
     obstipuit, retroque pedem cum voce repressit.
     improvisum aspris veluti qui sentibus anguem
230   pressit humi nitens, trepidusque repente refugit
     attollentem iras et caerula colla tumentem:
     haud secus Androgeos visu tremefactus abibat.
     inruimus densis et circumfundimur armis,
     ignarosque loci passim et formidine captos
235   sternimus. adspirat primo fortuna labori.

---

factus: literally *made to tremble.* **abibat:** Note the special use of the imperfect tense – *began to move away.*

233 **circumfundimur:** Supply **eos** (i.e. Androgeos and his men). This is another use of the Passive to imitate the Greek Middle Voice. (Compare lines 107 and 158.) The Passive is used reflexively as the equivalent of **nos circumfundimus,** *we pour round*; the Passive is then given an object of its own – *we pour round them* (LN # 20).

234 **ignaros:** agrees with **eos** (understood) in line 233.

235 **labori:** dative with **adspirat:** *our efforts.*

236 **hic:** *at this point.*   **animis:** Although both ablatives go with **exsultans**, this word is most neatly translated *in high spirits.*

237 **qua:** *where.*   **salutis:** Take with **iter.** Although it is genitive, we would say *the road to safety.*

238 **dextra:** nominative agreeing with the subject of **ostendit** (i.e. **fortuna**), where more naturally it might have been **dextram** agreeing with **se.** Things that were seen *on the right* were regarded as *favourable*; contrast things seen on the left which were thought of as a bad omen (**sinister**).   **sequamur:** present subjunctive expressing an exhortation – *let us follow.* (So also **mutemus** and **aptemus.**)

239 **insignia:** These were the marks or special features of the armour and weapons which distinguished one army from another. (Cf. the heraldic signs of the Middle Ages.) Here the word stands for the *armour and weapons* themselves.

240 **dolus an virtus:** Supply **utrum sit** at the beginning – an indirect question depending on **requirat.** Compare our expression *All's fair in love and war.* **requirat:** Who *would* (*bother to*) *ask?*, i.e. *who cares?*

241 **ipsi:** (*The Greeks*) *themselves*, i.e. those who had just been killed.

242 **clipei insigne decorum:** literally *the beautiful badge of the shield*, i.e. *the shield with its beautiful markings.*

243 **induitur:** Although Passive, it imitates the Greek Middle Voice (cf. lines 107, 158 and 233) which can take a direct object. Translate *he put on.* (LN # 20)

245 **recentibus:** because they had been newly captured.

246 **haud numine nostro:** *under the protection of a power* (i.e. god) *that was not really ours.* By wearing the Greek arms they theoretically came under the protection of gods who would normally protect Greeks, not Trojans.

248 **Orco:** dative, where prose would have used **ad Orcum.** Orcus was one of the names given to Hades, which here symbolises *death.*

249 **cursu petunt:** literally *they sought with their running*, i.e. *they ran towards.*

250 **fida:** *safe* (i.e. a place they could trust). There was a stockade round the ships which they had beached on the shore.   **pars:** Compare line 20. Note the verb is plural, following the sense of **pars.** (Cf. **mirantur** in line 21.)

251 **nota alvo:** There is a touch of irony in this description: they feared the attacking Trojans so much that they even climbed back into the horse to get away from them.   **conduntur:** another passive used reflexively (LN # 20).

252 **nihil fas:** Supply **est.** **nihil** is used adverbially: literally *it is not at all allowed.* The subject of **fas est** is the accusative and infinitive

19 A plan to deceive the Greeks

In an attempt to deceive the enemy, we decided to exchange our own armour for that of the Greeks whom we had killed.

atque hic successu exsultans animisque Coroebus
"o socii, qua prima" inquit "fortuna salutis
monstrat iter, quaque ostendit se dextra, sequamur:
mutemus clipeos, Danaumque insignia nobis
240   aptemus.   dolus an virtus, quis in hoste requirat?
arma dabunt ipsi."   sic fatus deinde comantem
Androgei galeam clipeique insigne decorum
induitur, laterique Argivum accommodat ensem.
hoc Rhipeus, hoc ipse Dymas, omnisque iuventus
245   laeta facit; spoliis se quisque recentibus armat.
vadimus inmixti Danais haud numine nostro.
multaque per caecam congressi proelia noctem
conserimus.   multos Danaum demittimus Orco.
diffugiunt alii ad naves, et litora cursu
250   fida petunt; pars ingentem formidine turpi
scandunt rursus equum, et nota conduntur in alvo.

20 Things go wrong

All went well for a time, until we went to the rescue of Cassandra who was being carried off in chains. Alas! Our own men thought we were enemies.

heu nihil invitis fas quemquam fidere divis!
ecce trahebatur passis Priameia virgo

---

quemquam fidere – literally *that anyone trust*.   **divis** is dative depending on **fidere**.   **invitis** is used predicatively, *if they are unwilling*. Translate *no one may put any trust in the gods if they are against him*.

253 **passis crinibus:** Ablative of Instrument, *by her dishevelled hair* (LN # 12).   **Priameia virgo:** *the unwed daughter of Priam*, in apposition to **Cassandra** in the next line.

254 **adytis:** poetic plural. The **adytum** was the inner shrine within the **templum**, making this an even greater crime since it was usually recognised that a person who sought sanctuary in a temple might not be harmed while there.

255 **ardentia:** *fiery*; such a look in her eyes describes the anger and defiance she displayed.

256 **arcebant:** The verb **arcere** means *to prevent one from reaching something one wishes to reach.* Here it means *prevented* her from holding her palms up to heaven, which was the customary thing to do in prayer.

257 **non tulit:** literally *did not endure*, i.e. he found it too much for him to bear.

258 **periturus:** nominative of the future participle agreeing with subject of **iniecit** – *doomed to die.*

261 **nostrorum:** *of our own men*, who mistook them for Greeks.
obruimur: Although the last syllable is short in quantity, Virgil has chosen to make it long because of the stress before the strong break in the line.

262 **armorum facie:** *(resulting) from the appearance of the armour.*

263 **ereptae virginis ira:** literally *with anger (the result) of the snatched maiden*; we would say *angry at the rescue of the maiden*. Actually, it was only an attempted rescue.

264 **acerrimus:** Ajax was *fiercest of all* because he had been the captor of Cassandra.

265 **gemini Atridae**: *the two sons of Atreus*, Agamemnon and Menelaus. They were brothers but not twins. For the form **Atridae** cf. lines 52, 66, 148.

266 **numero:** *by weight of numbers.*

267 **iustissimus unus:** *easily the most upright, far and away the most upright.*

269 **a sociis:** They were still clad in the Greek armour.   **tua plurima pietas:** *your great goodness.* For **pietas** see AIC 128.

270 **infula:** *a fillet*, i.e. a woollen headband worn by priests, with woollen strands hanging from it. One might have expected it to have protected him from attack.

271 **sedes:** poetic plural.

272 **ad tecta ruentes:** *attempting to storm the walls* (lit. *rushing to the roof-tops*).

273 **acta testudine:** *by soldiers attacking with their shields locked above their heads.* One method of attacking a fortress was for troops to advance in close formation with their shields above their heads. The

crinibus a templo Cassandra adytisque Minervae,
255   ad caelum tendens ardentia lumina frustra,
lumina, nam teneras arcebant vincula palmas.
non tulit hanc speciem furiata mente Coroebus,
et sese medium iniecit periturus in agmen.
consequimur cuncti et densis incurrimus armis.
260   hic primum ex alto delubri culmine telis
nostrorum obruimur, oriturque miserrima caedes
armorum facie et Graiarum errore iubarum.
tum Danai gemitu atque ereptae virginis ira
undique collecti invadunt, acerrimus Aiax,
265   et gemini Atridae, Dolopumque exercitus omnis.
ilicet obruimur numero: primusque Coroebus
procumbit; cadit et Rhipeus, iustissimus unus
qui fuit in Teucris; pereunt Hypanisque Dymasque
confixi a sociis; nec te tua plurima, Panthu,
270   labentem pietas, nec Apollinis infula texit.

21 An attempt to save Priam's palace

Next we tried to drive off the Greeks who were attacking
Priam's palace. As the Greeks tried to scale the walls, the
Trojans hurled down weapons at them and also toppled
masonry on their heads.

protinus ad sedes Priami clamore vocati,
ingentem pugnam Danaosque ad tecta ruentes
cernimus, obsessumque acta testudine limen.
haerent parietibus scalae, postesque sub ipsos

---

tortoise-like shell protected them against weapons thrown from the
walls.

274 **parietibus:** Note the scansion; the first **-i-** is treated as a consonant
and sounded 'y' (as in 'yes').

275 **nituntur gradibus:** literally *they struggled by the rungs (of the ladders)*, i.e. *they tried to force their way up the rungs.*

276 **protecti:** Passive used as a reflexive (see lines 107 and 233) – *protecting themselves* (LN # 20). **clipeos ad tela sinistris obiciunt:** literally *with their left hands they presented their shields towards (against) the weapons*, i.e. *they protected themselves by holding up their shields with their left hands against the weapons.*

277 **contra:** Used adverbially – *in opposition, fighting back.*
tecta: literally *roofs*, i.e. *tiles.*

278 **imas fores:** *the doors below.*

279 **obsedere** = **obsederunt**. Normally, we associate the verb **obsidere** with besieging from the outside; here, it is used of the Trojans blocking the door from the inside. **has:** Supply **fores**.

280 **instaurati animi:** Supply **sunt**: *our spirits were renewed*, i.e. they were eager again, which explains the use of the infinitive. *This gave us fresh heart to . . .*

281 **vim:** *strength*. Note the alliteration in this line: the letter **v** appears four times (LN # 33).

282 **evado:** *I climbed up.*

284 **in praecipiti:** *on the edge (of the battlements).*

285 **sedibus:** poetic plural – *from its position*. **impulimus:** Note the change from the historic present (LN # 22) to the perfect tense to show the suddenness of this action. **ea:** *it*, the tower. **ruinam trahit:** A vivid way of describing what happens when a structure like a tower or tall chimney falls; as the top part falls, it seems to gather up the parts beneath it and drag them with it, like an avalanche.

287 **incidit:** Note the effect of the strong break after the single word (cf. lines 222 and 228), which adds even more effect to the words which follow; the situation is hopeless.

288 **cessat:** *flagged*, i.e. missiles of all kinds kept coming thick and fast. This is another line which Virgil left unfinished. (Cf. lines 46 and 121.)

289 **vestibulum:** Virgil describes Priam's palace as if it were designed in the same way as a Roman house. The **vestibulum** was the short passage leading from the street to the door, which was not at the street but recessed slightly. The **limen** was the actual doorway. **-que:** *and then*. **primo in limine:** *in the very entrance*. **Pyrrhus:** the son of Achilles, called Neoptolemus in line 148.

290 **telis et luce coruscus aena:** literally *glittering with weapons and bronze light*, i.e. *gleaming with the glint of his bronze armour* (Hendiadys: LN # 27). The word **coruscus** describes not only the glint from the armour but also the exhilaration he felt in victory. He was showing off (**exsultat**). **aena:** three syllables **a-e-na**.

275 nituntur gradibus, clipeosque ad tela sinistris
protecti obiciunt, prensant fastigia dextris.
Dardanidae contra turres ac tecta domorum
devolvunt; alii strictis mucronibus imas
obsedere fores; has servant agmine denso.
280 instaurati animi regis succurrere tectis
auxilioque levare viros vimque addere victis.
evado ad summi fastigia culminis, unde
tela manu miseri iactabant irrita Teucri.
turrim in praecipiti stantem convellimus altis
285 sedibus, impulimusque. ea lapsa repente ruinam
cum sonitu trahit, et Danaum super agmina late
incidit. ast alii subeunt; nec saxa nec ullum
telorum interea cessat genus.

22 The Greeks break into the palace

Pyrrhus at last broke through the door and swept into the
palace, murdering the guards. The women cowered in fear.

vestibulum ante ipsum primoque in limine Pyrrhus
290 exsultat, telis et luce coruscus aena.
una ingens Periphas et equorum agitator Achillis
armiger Automedon, una omnis Scyria pubes
succedunt tecto, et flammas ad culmina iactant.
ipse inter primos correpta dura bipenni
295 limina perrumpit, postesque a cardine vellit.
apparet domus intus, et atria longa patescunt;

---

291 **una:** *along with him.*

292 **Scyria pubes:** Pyrrhus came from the island of Scyros. For the
meaning of **pubes**, compare the use of **iuventus** in AIC 299. Translate *all his warriors from Scyros.* Note the plural verb.

294 **ipse:** i.e. Pyrrhus. Scan the line to discover whether the final -a is
long in **correpta** and **dura**. This will help you to take these words
with the correct nouns.

297 The repetition of the verb **apparere** adds emphasis to the violation of the privacy of the ancient palace.

298 **armatos vident: armatos** refers to the Trojans who were grouping themselves immediately inside the door (**in limine primo**); the subject of **vident** is the attacking Greeks. This whole scene is described from the standpoint of the Greeks who were standing in the open doorway.

299 **domus interior:** literally *the inner house*, i.e. *the inside of the palace.* This probably means the same as **domus intus** in line 296, but notice that **intus** is an adverb while **interior** is an adjective.

300 **miscetur:** *was in confusion*; see AIC 100 for the basic meaning of this verb. **penitus:** *deep inside* (*the palace*), i.e. within the private living quarters. **cavae aedes:** The halls are called hollow because they were *vaulted.*

301 **ululant:** *wailed.* The word itself imitates the echoing sound, so that it appears as if the walls themselves are wailing.
ferit: literally *struck*, i.e. *rose as high as.*

302 **tectis ingentibus:** omission of preposition (see LN # 1). Note also the poetic plural.

303 They were clinging to the home they loved, realising that they were about to be parted from it.

304 **patria:** an adjective; his father was Achilles.

305 **sufferre:** Supply **eum.** **ariete crebro:** *under* (literally *from*) *the frequent* (*blows of the*) *battering-ram.* Scan **ariete** as three syllables, since the **-i-** is treated as a consonant. (Cf. line 274.)

306 **emoti cardine:** A **cardo** was not like a modern hinge. In a double door there was, at the extreme right and extreme left, a stout post (**postis**) which protruded above and below the rest of the door. The ends of the **postis** were set in sockets (**cardines**) in the lintel and in the floor so that the door turned in these pivot-holes. Under the force of the ram, the **postes** were forced out of the sockets (**emoti**) and, since they were an integral part of the door, the door fell.

307 **fit via vi:** Brief and to the point! Again, the strong break in the second foot stresses the relentless onslaught, only momentarily held up by the door. Note how expressive these simple words are after the struggle (described in spondees in line 306). **rumpunt aditus:** literally *they burst an entrance* (**aditus** is poetic plural), i.e. *they forced their way in.* **primos:** *the first* (*guards*).

308 **milite:** a collective singular for plural (cf. line 9 and LN # 3).

309 **non sic:** another way of introducing a simile. Literally *not like this*, i.e. the onslaught of Pyrrhus was far more violent than a river bursting its banks. (LN # 26)

apparent Priami et veterum penetralia regum,
armatosque vident stantes in limine primo.
at domus interior gemitu miseroque tumultu
300 miscetur; penitusque cavae plangoribus aedes
femineis ululant; ferit aurea sidera clamor.
tum pavidae tectis matres ingentibus errant,
amplexaeque tenent postes, atque oscula figunt.
instat vi patria Pyrrhus; nec claustra neque ipsi
305 custodes sufferre valent.   labat ariete crebro
ianua, et emoti procumbunt cardine postes.
fit via vi: rumpunt aditus, primosque trucidant
inmissi Danai, et late loca milite complent.
non sic, aggeribus ruptis cum spumeus amnis
310 exiit, oppositasque evicit gurgite moles,
fertur in arva furens cumulo, camposque per omnes
cum stabulis armenta trahit.   vidi ipse furentem
caede Neoptolemum, geminosque in limine Atridas:
vidi Hecubam centumque nurus, Priamumque per aras
315 sanguine foedantem quos ipse sacraverat ignes.

---

310 **exiit:** Note the perfect which emphasises that it is the very moment
when the river has burst its banks with which the comparison is
made (cf. **evicit**). In the next sentence, however, he reverts to the
present tense to describe the river sweeping along.   **oppositasque:** In
this context, **-que** does not mean *and*; rather it introduces another
description of the same scene, *namely*, the bursting of the banks.
(Cf. AIC 24 and 34.) (LN # 37)   **moles:** Compare line 21. Here
moles means the *barrier of earth* which forms the *banks*.

311 **cumulo:** literally *in a heap*, i.e. *in a wall of water*. (Cf. AIC 51.)

312 **trahit:** literally *draws along*; we would tend to say *sweeps along*.
vidi ipse: Although it is Aeneas who is describing the whole scene,
the use of **vidi** in the next part of the sentence is all the more
poignant as the victims were his own kith and kin.   **furentem
caede:** *crazed with the killing* or *mad with the lust for blood*.

314 **centum nurus:** Priam was said to have had fifty sons, all of them
married, and fifty daughters. In this moment of crisis, the *hundred
princesses* (fifty daughters and fifty daughters-in-law) had gathered
round Queen Hecuba.   **per aras:** *among the altars*.

315 **quos:** The antecedent is **ignes**.

85

316 **quinquaginta thalami:** Each of the married sons had a marriage-chamber in the palace. **illi:** *those famous.* **spes tanta nepotum: spes** is in apposition to **thalami**. Translate *which held such great hopes for continuing the family line.*

317 **barbarico:** The Greeks looked upon all non-Greeks as *barbarian*, and Roman writers sometimes used the word in the same sense even though, as here, it is a non-Greek who is speaking. Translate *foreign*. **postes:** The **thalami** and **postes** are both subjects of **procubuere:** the doors fell (literally) and the rooms fell (metaphorically). **auro spoliisque:** Take these words closely with **superbi** – *proud with the spoils of (foreign) gold.*

318 **procubuere:** See line 61. **qua deficit ignis:** literally *where the fire failed*, i.e. *the parts which the fire failed to reach.* The verb **tenent** has no object in the Latin, but this clause almost acts like an object. In effect, the Trojans had nowhere to run to; part of the house was on fire and the rest was held by the Greeks.

319 **forsitan requiras:** *perhaps you may ask.* **requiras** is subjunctive depending on **forsitan**. Remember that Aeneas is speaking to Dido. **et:** *also.* **Priami fuerint quae fata** is an indirect question depending on **requiras**. **fata:** poetic plural.

320 **uti = ut:** *when.* **convulsa** is used predicatively. (LN # 36)

321 **tectorum:** poetic plural. **medium:** Although this adjective agrees with **hostem,** English would more naturally take it with **in penetralibus:** *in the middle of the living quarters.* (Transferred Epithet: LN # 14)

322 **senior:** Although this word may be translated as the equivalent of **senex**, the use of the comparative suggests that he was *too old* to fight. The 'old man' is, of course, Priam. This line and the next are packed with allusions to the hopelessness of what he is trying: **senior, arma diu desueta, trementibus aevo umeris, nequiquam** and **inutile ferrum. arma:** *armour.*

323 **umeris:** dative depending on **circumdat.** **ferrum cingitur:** For the use of the accusative with a passive verb compare line 158. Translate *he fastened (to himself) his sword.* (LN # 20)

324 **fertur:** *he began to go forward* or *he was making his way.* **moriturus:** *intent on dying* or *resolved to fight to the death.*

325 **aedibus in mediis:** Like the Roman house which had an **atrium** with an opening in the roof and a **peristylium** surrounded by a colonnade, Priam's palace had a 'hall' which was really a courtyard open to the sky. In it there was an altar to Zeus. **axe** describes the curved effect of the sky: *vault.* Remember that the ancients thought the sky was a huge sphere which encircled the earth (cf. line 138).

327 **natae:** They weren't all her daughters. See line 314. **circum:** preposition governing **altaria.**

quinquaginta illi thalami, spes tanta nepotum,
barbarico postes auro spoliisque superbi
procubuere: tenent Danai qua deficit ignis.

23 A vain gesture

Poor old Priam! When he saw his palace invaded, he
strapped on his armour which he had not worn for years
and made ready to die fighting. Hecuba, however,
persuaded him to join her and her daughters beside an altar
where they might be safe. But Pyrrhus was no respecter of
altars.

     forsitan et, Priami fuerint quae fata, requiras.
320 urbis uti captae casum convulsaque vidit
     limina tectorum, et medium in penetralibus hostem,
     arma diu senior desueta trementibus aevo
     circumdat nequiquam umeris, et inutile ferrum
     cingitur, ac densos fertur moriturus in hostes.
325 aedibus in mediis nudoque sub aetheris axe
     ingens ara fuit iuxtaque veterrima laurus.
     hic Hecuba et natae nequiquam altaria circum,
     praecipites atra ceu tempestate columbae,
     condensae et divom amplexae simulacra sedebant.
330 ipsum autem sumptis Priamum iuvenilibus armis

---

328 **ceu:** yet another way of introducing a simile. (Compare lines 111,
179 and 229.) (LN # 26) **praecipites:** (*driven*) *headlong.*

329 **divom:** For added protection they were clasping hold of the statues
of the gods on the altar. (See LN # 5.)

330 **autem:** the storytelling *now*, used to direct the attention of the
reader back to Priam. **iuvenilibus:** not *juvenile* but *manly*,
i.e. suited to someone in his prime. (See AIC 299.) **sumptis iuvenilibus armis** is an ablative absolute. English would most naturally use
an expression like *dressed in*.

331 **ut vidit:** The subject is **Hecuba.** **quae mens tam dira:** *What crazy thought;* English does not translate the idiomatic **tam.**

332 **impulit:** Supply **te.** **cingi:** For the passive used reflexively see LN # 20: *to gird oneself.* Note that, unlike line 323, an ablative (**telis**) is used here.

333 **non tali. . . nec istis:** Hecuba means that they must now put their faith in the gods; not even Hector could save them now by fighting. When using these words, she would point to the armour that Priam has just put on. The word **istis** may be used scornfully, but it is more likely that Hecuba used it with tenderness and pity.

334 **tempus:** *our situation* or *our predicament.* **non:** From the previous part of the sentence (**non tali . . . eget**) it is necessary to supply the main clause of this conditional sentence: *the situation would not need . . ., even if Hector were here* (**adforet** = **adesset**).

335 **tandem:** *at last,* a sign of impatience implying *it is high time* or *before it is too late.*

336 **moriere** is another form of **morieris.** **sic ore effata:** See line 38 (LN # 39). **ore:** literally *with her mouth,* but it is probably unnecessary to translate it in English. If, on the other hand, you think Virgil is contrasting what she said and what she was thinking, translate it *this is what she said out loud.* **recepit:** Supply **eum,** or **longaevum** (from the next clause).

337 **sacra in sede:** i.e. near the altar.

338 **Pyrrhi de caede:** literally *from the slaughter of Pyrrhus,* i.e. the slaughter inflicted by Pyrrhus.

339 **per tela, per hostes:** The repetition of **per** creates the impression of the effort involved in making the escape. The theme is continued in the next line. It must have seemed to the wounded man that he would never reach safety; he had to run the gauntlet of weapons and enemies, on and on down the long colonnades and through the empty halls.

341 **saucius:** Note the effect of delaying this word to the end of the sentence, together with the impact it makes because of the strong caesura in the second foot. **ardens insequitur:** *hotly pursued.* **infesto vulnere:** literally *with hostile wound.* Translate *threatening to strike.*

342 **iam iamque:** The repetition of **iam** – fairly common in Virgil – indicates that he is so close to him that time and time again he appears to be on the point of catching him. Translate *time and time again, on the point of. . .*

343 **ante oculos et ora:** *before the eyes and gaze* (literally *faces*).

344 **concidit:** Again, a dramatic effect is produced by the strong caesura in the second foot.

ut vidit, "quae mens tam dira, miserrime coniunx,
impulit his cingi telis?   aut quo ruis?" inquit.
"non tali auxilio, nec defensoribus istis
tempus eget; non, si ipse meus nunc adforet Hector.
335   huc tandem concede; haec ara tuebitur omnes,
aut moriere simul."   sic ore effata recepit
ad sese, et sacra longaevum in sede locavit.
ecce autem elapsus Pyrrhi de caede Polites,
unus natorum Priami, per tela, per hostes,
340   porticibus longis fugit, et vacua atria lustrat
saucius.   illum ardens infesto vulnere Pyrrhus
insequitur, iam iamque manu tenet et premit hasta.
ut tandem ante oculos evasit et ora parentum,
concidit, ac multo vitam cum sanguine fudit.

24 A rebuke for Pyrrhus

Priam upbraided Pyrrhus as being unworthy of his father,
Achilles; and as a gesture of defiance he hurled his spear
weakly at him.

345   hic Priamus, quamquam in media iam morte tenetur,
non tamen abstinuit, nec voci iraeque pepercit:
"di tibi pro scelere" exclamat "pro talibus ausis
persolvant grates dignas, et praemia reddant

---

345 **hic:** *at this moment.*   **in media morte tenetur:** literally *he was held
in the midst of death*, i.e. *he was in the clutches of death*, meaning
that his fate was sealed.

346 **nec voci iraeque pepercit:** literally *and he did not spare his voice and
his anger.* Translate *and he lashed out with angry tongue* or *and he
gave full vent to his angry words.* (Hendiadys: LN # 27)

347 **di persolvant:** The present subjunctive expresses a wish – *may the
gods pay in full.*

348 **praemia reddant debita:** *may they give you a just reward*, a reward
that fits what you did; in this case, evil for evil. Notice that **reddere**
here does not mean *to give back* but *to give what you deserve*, i.e.
basically the same notion as **debita**.

349 **qui:** The antecedent is **tibi** which explains the ending of **fecisti** (*you*) *who have forced me to witness.*

350 **foedasti** = **foedavisti** (LN # 18). **vultus:** poetic plural: *sight* or *eyes.* It would have been bad enough to commit this sort of murder at any time, but the fact that it was done in front of his own father made it really cruel.

351 **ille Achilles:** *the famous Achilles.* **satum quo te mentiris:** Supply **esse** with **satum te** (accusative and infinitive) depending on **mentiris.** The ablative **quo** means *from whom*; literally *from whom you lie that you have been born,* i.e. *whose son you falsely claim to be.* It is a taunt to the effect that he is unworthy of his father.

352 **non talis in hoste fuit:** literally *was not such a man in (the case of) an enemy,* i.e. *did not behave like this towards an enemy.* After Achilles had slain Hector and dragged his body round the walls of Troy behind his chariot, he showed some chivalry in allowing Priam to ransom the body and take it back to Troy for a decent burial. **iura fidemque supplicis erubuit:** *Blushing* is a sign of conscience. Suppliants had certain rights, but only if the other person was honourable. Certainly, Priam took a risk in entering the Greek camp in order to plead with Achilles and had to show some trust (**fides**) in his sense of honour. Translate *he respected a suppliant's rights to protection.*

353 **sepulchro:** literally *to the tomb,* i.e. *for burial.*

354 **regna:** poetic plural.

355 **sic fatus:** See line 38 for this story-telling convention. (LN # 39) Supply **est** with **fatus.** **sine ictu:** literally *without a blow,* i.e. it was too weak to *wound* him. Translate *harmlessly.*

356 **coniecit:** Again, note how effective the strong pause in the second foot after the single word can be. **repulsum:** Supply **est.**

357 **summo umbone:** The shield was made of wood and leather. In the centre was a bronze boss, also covered with leather, which was intended to deflect weapons. Priam's spear was thrown so weakly that it was able only to pierce the leather covering but could not penetrate the metal below. Translate (*it hung*) *from the leather covering of the boss.*

358 **cui Pyrrhus:** Supply **inquit.** **cui** is a Linking Relative = *to him.* **ergo:** *therefore* is used because of all the distasteful things he has said and tried to do to Pyrrhus. In other words, Pyrrhus feels he has deserved it. **referes haec:** *you will carry this tale.* Like **reddant** in line 348, **referre** does not mean *to carry back* but to carry it to the proper person. The future is the equivalent of a command here. (Compare the Ten Commandments.) **nuntius** is used predicatively (LN # 36).

debita, qui nati coram me cernere letum
350 fecisti, et patrios foedasti funere vultus.
at non ille, satum quo te mentiris, Achilles
talis in hoste fuit Priamo; sed iura fidemque
supplicis erubuit, corpusque exsangue sepulchro
reddidit Hectoreum, meque in mea regna remisit."
355 sic fatus senior, telumque imbelle sine ictu
coniecit, rauco quod protinus aere repulsum,
et summo clipei nequiquam umbone pependit.

25 Priam is slain

Pyrrhus mocked him and then slew him, showing no mercy
for his age.

cui Pyrrhus "referes ergo haec, et nuntius ibis
Pelidae genitori. illi mea tristia facta
360 degeneremque Neoptolemum narrare memento.
nunc morere!" hoc dicens, altaria ad ipsa trementem
traxit et in multo lapsantem sanguine nati;

---

359 **illi:** *to him* – emphatic.

360 **narrare** is used with two constructions here: (a) the direct object
tristia facta; (b) the accusative and infinitive **degenerem (esse)
Neoptolemum**.

361 **morere** is the imperative of **morior**. **hoc dicens:** Compare line 355.
The present participle indicates that the actions which are described in lines 361–364 were carried out while he was speaking, so
making the scene even more blood-thirsty. **altaria:** poetic plural.
trementem agrees with **Priamum** (understood). Compare **lapsantem**.

362 **in multo sanguine:** *in a pool of blood*. Note how Virgil builds up the
cruelty and the pathos. The weak old man is already no match for
the young Pyrrhus, but he is even more handicapped because he
can't even keep his footing, and the irony of it is that Priam's son,
even in death, contributes to his father's death.

363 Scan the line to discover the case of **laeva** and **dextra**. Note the effect of putting these two words next to each other. Victory is all too easy for Pyrrhus. **coruscum** agrees with **ensem** in line 364.

364 **lateri abdidit:** *buried . . . in his side.* The dative **lateri** replaces the more natural **in latus**.

365 **circumstetit:** literally *stood around me,* i.e. *was brought home to me.*

366 **obstipui:** Again, note the very powerful pause in the second foot after the single word. (Cf. line 356.) **subiit imago:** literally *the picture sprang up,* i.e. *I suddenly thought of.*

367 **aequaevum:** Aeneas' father was *the same age* as Priam.

368 **subiit deserta Creusa:** This obviously refers to his suddenly remembering about Creusa whom he had left behind at home. (Cf. line 366.)

369 **direpta domus:** Aeneas' home had not yet been plundered, but the sight of the plundered palace conjured up in his mind a picture of his own house in ruins.

370 **omne:** emphatic, agreeing with **Ilium. visum:** Supply **est.**

371 **Neptunia Troia:** According to legend, Neptune had helped to build the walls of Troy for King Laomedon, who then refused to pay. **ex imo:** *from its lowest* (*part*), i.e. *from its foundations.* There are two pictures of the destruction, one of buildings being engulfed in flames, the other of buildings crashing into their foundations.

372 **ducente deo:** an ablative absolute. Although **deo** is masculine, it is undoubtedly Venus he means. Translate *with a deity to guide me, because a deity was guiding me,* which explains why his path was so easy. **inter** governs **flammam** as well as **hostes.** Note that **flammam** is singular where the plural might have been more natural. The singular has the effect of suggesting that he had to do this repeatedly.

373 **dant tela locum:** *weapons gave way* (*before me*), i.e. his opponents were forced back as he fought his way through their midst.

374 **ubi perventum:** Supply **est.** This impersonal passive expression means literally *when it was come;* English would say *when I came* or *when the doorway was reached.* **limina:** poetic plural. (Compare also **domos.**)

377 **excisa Troia:** ablative absolute, giving his reason for refusing.

378 **si voluissent. . . ., servassent:** *if* (*they*) *had wished . . . . ., they would have saved . . .* **servassent** is the shortened form of **servavissent.** Note the emphatic position of **me.**

implicuitque comam laeva, dextraque coruscum
extulit ac lateri capulo tenus abdidit ensem.

26 Aeneas comes to his senses

The shock of seeing Priam murdered brought Aeneas to
his senses. He suddenly thought of his own family whom
he had left behind unprotected. He fought his way back to
them, guided by his mother, Venus.

365   at me tum primum saevus circumstetit horror.
      obstipui. subiit cari genitoris imago,
      ut regem aequaevum crudeli vulnere vidi
      vitam exhalantem; subiit deserta Creusa,
      et direpta domus, et parvi casus Iuli.
370   tum vero omne mihi visum considere in ignes
      Ilium, et ex imo verti Neptunia Troia.
      descendo, ac ducente deo flammam inter et hostes
      expedior. dant tela locum, flammaeque recedunt.

27 A stubborn old man

When I reached home, my father refused to leave. He kept
saying that he had lived long enough and did not wish to
survive the destruction of his home and his country.
Nothing my wife and I said could persuade him to go.

      atque ubi iam patriae perventum ad limina sedis
375   antiquasque domos, genitor, quem tollere in altos
      optabam primum montes primumque petebam,
      abnegat excisa vitam producere Troia.
      "me si caelicolae voluissent ducere vitam,

379 **sedes:** poetic plural. In line 374 the singular was used. **satis una superque vidimus excidia:** To understand this, take **vidimus** separately with **satis superque** (*I have seen enough and more than enough*) and then with **una excidia** (*I have seen one destruction*); then put the two expressions together – *I have seen enough and more than enough in seeing one destruction.* There are several other points worth noting. Firstly, the plural *we* for *I* is common in poetry. Secondly, **excidia** is poetic plural, and agreeing with it is an unusual plural of **unus, -a, -um.**

380 **una excidia:** After Laomedon had refused to reward Neptune for building the walls of Troy, Neptune sent a sea-monster to seize his daughter, Hesione. Hercules agreed to save the girl by slaying the monster. Laomedon again broke his word and Hercules attacked the city, destroyed it and killed Laomedon. Anchises says that he survived that destruction and has no desire to survive another. **captae superavimus urbi:** This continues the same idea of the previous clause. In lines 108 and 178, you learned that the basic idea of **superare** is *to be above.* In this line, the same basic idea exists. It is the idea of the victor standing over the vanquished. In this case, Anchises is still alive (and standing), while the city is captured and in ruins. Translate **superavimus** as *I have survived.* Note that it governs the dative. English would naturally translate **captae urbi** *the capture of the city* (literally *the captured city.*)

381 **manu:** He does not mean that he will commit suicide, as is made clear by the rest of the sentence. He will be killed trying to fight the enemy and, since he realises that resistance is hopeless, he will, in effect, be responsible for his own death. **miserebitur:** He does not mean that the enemy will spare him through pity but they *will put me out of my misery.* Note the alliteration: the letter 'm' appears five times in this line (LN # 33).

382 **exuvias:** *my armour as spoil.* **facilis:** (*is*) *easy* (*to bear*). **iactura sepulchri:** *the loss of proper burial.* Only someone who had reached the depths of despair would say such a thing since, as far as people in antiquity were concerned, the worst fate that could befall someone was to be left unburied and thus not gain access to the underworld.

383 **talia:** Compare line 38 (LN # 39). **talia** is the object of **memorans.**

384 **in arma feror:** The context shows that he did not actually rush out into battle, but *felt the urge to return to the battle.*

385 **quod consilium dabatur:** *What was the point of making plans?* The gods had already decided our fate. **dare** is used in the sense *to offer.* (Literally *what plan was offered?*) **fortuna:** *chance* (*of escaping*).

387 **lux ultima:** *the last day.*

has mihi servassent sedes. satis una superque
380 vidimus excidia, et captae superavimus urbi.
ipse manu mortem inveniam; miserebitur hostis
exuviasque petet. facilis iactura sepulchri."
talia perstabat memorans, fixusque manebat.

28 An omen

I decided to return to the battle; if we were to die, at least
we would die fighting. Creusa was appealing to me not to
leave them unprotected when a strange thing happened to
Iulus.

rursus in arma feror, mortemque miserrimus opto.
385 nam quod consilium aut quae iam fortuna dabatur?
"si nihil ex tanta superis placet urbe relinqui,
arma, viri, ferte arma! vocat lux ultima victos.
reddite me Danais! sinite instaurata revisam
proelia! numquam omnes hodie moriemur inulti."
390 hinc ferro accingor rursus, clipeoque sinistram
insertabam aptans, meque extra tecta ferebam.
ecce autem complexa pedes in limine coniunx

---

388 **sinite instaurata revisam proelia:** *let me return to the battle and fight
once more.* **sinere** may be used with the infinitive or with **ut** and
the subjunctive. In poetry, the **ut** may be omitted. (Literally *allow
me to revisit the renewed battle.*)

389 **numquam** has no time sense here; it is an emphatic way of
expressing *not.*

390 **clipeo sinistram insertabam aptans:** Literally *I was inserting my left
arm, fitting it to the shield.* There were two straps behind the shield,
one in the middle under which the arm was passed and one near the
rim which was held in the hand. Translate *I was slipping my left arm
under the strap of the shield.*

391 **me ferebam:** *I was making my way.*

392 **complexa pedes:** It was customary for a suppliant to grasp the knees
of the person to whom the request was being made. In this case,
Creusa was also trying to stop him leaving the palace.

393 **patri:** Note how Virgil says *to his father* (i.e. Aeneas) rather than *to me* since it is to his love as a father that she is appealing.

394 **periturus:** The future participle denotes *determined to die* (cf. line 258). **et nos:** *us also.* **in omnia:** literally *into everything*, i.e. *into whatever fate awaits you.*

395 **expertus:** *having tried* (*arms* understood).

397 **coniunx quondam tua dicta:** *once called your wife.* By abandoning her he was, as it were, renouncing his marriage vow to cherish her till death parted them. **relinquor:** The verb agrees with the nearest subject; with **Iulus** and **pater** understand **relinquitur.**

398 **talia:** Compare line 38. (LN # 39)

399 **monstrum:** *sign* or *portent.* The word has the same derivation as the verb *monstrare.* The notion of *monster* came later, anything weird being regarded as a sign sent by the gods.

400 **inter** governs **manus** and **ora.** Remember that Creusa was on her knees, holding Iulus up to Aeneas.

401 **levis apex:** *a flickering tongue of flame.* Supply **est** with **visus.** The flame was regarded by Anchises as a sign that some favourable deity was present to signify that Iulus would have a glorious future. He was, of course, to become the founder of the **gens Iulia**, the family to which Julius Caesar and the Emperor Augustus belonged. The *Aeneid* was written in the reign of Augustus to glorify the magnificent achievements of Rome.

402 **tactu innoxia:** *harmless to touch*, i.e. it did him no harm. For the use of the ablative of the supine ending in **-u** used with adjectives compare **dictu mirabile** in line 399.

403 **flamma:** Supply **visa est.**

404 **trepidare, excutere** and **restinguere** are historic infinitives (cf. line 70) which are used to convey the excitement of a rapid series of events. They are translated as if they were past tenses of the indicative: *we anxiously leapt into action and tried to shake out and extinguish the flame.* (LN # 23)

407 **palmas:** Compare line 256. **cum voce:** *as he prayed.*

409 **aspice nos:** literally *behold us!* i.e. *pay attention to us!* **hoc tantum:** *this is my only prayer.* **pietate:** *by our goodness.*

410 **deinde:** Although, strictly speaking, this word is unnecessary, it adds considerable emphasis: if they have acted with reverence, then, automatically, they should be entitled to the help of the gods. **haec omina firma:** *confirm these signs* by sending a second sign to show that the first was not an accident.

412 **laevum:** *on the left.* Thunder heard on the left was a good sign as far as the Romans were concerned.

haerebat, parvumque patri tendebat Iulum:
"si periturus abis, et nos rape in omnia tecum.
395 sin aliquam expertus sumptis spem ponis in armis,
hanc primum tutare domum! cui parvus Iulus,
cui pater, et coniunx quondam tua dicta relinquor?"
talia vociferans gemitu tectum omne replebat;
cum subitum dictuque oritur mirabile monstrum.
400 namque manus inter maestorumque ora parentum
ecce levis summo de vertice visus Iuli
fundere lumen apex tactuque innoxia molles
lambere flamma comas, et circum tempora pasci.

29 Anchises convinced

We tried to beat out the flames, but Anchises hailed it as
a good omen and prayed to Jupiter for confirmation.
Immediately, two signs came and Anchises said he was now
ready to leave Troy.

nos pavidi trepidare metu crinemque flagrantem
405 excutere et sanctos restinguere fontibus ignes.
at pater Anchises oculos ad sidera laetus
extulit, et caelo palmas cum voce tetendit:
"Iuppiter omnipotens, precibus si flecteris ullis,
aspice nos – hoc tantum – et, si pietate meremur,
410 da deinde auxilium, pater, atque haec omina firma!"
vix ea fatus erat senior, subitoque fragore
intonuit laevum, et de caelo lapsa per umbras

line

413 **stella facem ducens:** *a star drawing a (tail of) fire*, i.e. a shooting star. **cucurrit:** *sped, shot.*

414 **hic vero:** *then indeed.* **victus:** *convinced, persuaded.* **ad auras:** literally *to the sky*, i.e. *upright.*

416 **nulla mora est:** He means that he is now not holding back. Translate *there is no reluctance (on my part).* Note how effectively the present tenses (**sequor** and **adsum**) convey his sense of urgency; he is not only prepared to go; he is on his way.

417 **domum:** *house* refers not to the building but to the race or family, as in the noble families of England, the House of York, etc. The idea is continued in **nepotem** which symbolises the future of their race.

418 **vestrum hoc augurium:** Supply **est.** **vestro in numine:** literally *in your power*, i.e. *under your protection.* **Troia:** Again, not the actual city which is being destroyed and appears to have been deserted by the gods, but the Trojan heritage which will continue through his son, Aeneas, and his grandson Iulus, wherever the new Troy is built.

419 **comes** is used predicatively. (LN # 36)

420 **dixerat:** For this epic convention, compare lines 38 and 63, (LN # 39). **moenia:** not *walls*, but *city*. **clarior ignis auditur:** The adjective **clarus** can be used to convey the *brightness* of things that are seen and the *loudness* or *clarity* of things that are heard. The two ideas are brought together here: the fire is raging more brightly but, because the fires are now very close at hand, the crackling can also be heard more distinctly.

421 **aestus:** poetic plural. **incendia** may also be poetic plural, but it may also refer to all the individual fires that have been started.

422 **imponere:** imperative passive, meaning literally *be placed upon.* It is used reflexively here: *place yourself upon*, i.e. *sit upon* (LN # 20). **nostrae:** *my.* Note how the short sentences convey the sense of speed and urgency.

424 **quo . . . cunque:** an example of Tmesis in which the two parts of the word are separated by another word (LN # 28). **res:** Although this may appear to be a weak and vague word, it can conjure up in the mind far more ideas than could be conveyed by more specific words like **fortuna** and **fatum**. For further examples, see AIC 87, 112, 172 and 180. **cadent:** The metaphor is that of the throwing of dice. Translate *however things turn out* or *whatever happens.*

426 **sit:** A jussive subjunctive, which gives an instruction: *let Iulus be.* **servet** is also jussive subjunctive: *let her follow.* **longe:** Presumably, his aim was to avoid attracting attention; the smaller the groups, the less likely they were to be noticed.

stella facem ducens multa cum luce cucurrit.
hic vero victus genitor se tollit ad auras,

415 adfaturque deos, et sanctum sidus adorat:
"iam iam nulla mora est. sequor et qua ducitis adsum,
di patrii. servate domum! servate nepotem!
vestrum hoc augurium, vestroque in numine Troia est.
cedo equidem. nec, nate, tibi comes ire recuso."

30 Plans for departure

I said I would carry Anchises on my back, with Iulus
walking at my side. For safety, Creusa would follow. We
fixed a rendezvous at the gates.

420 dixerat ille. et iam per moenia clarior ignis
auditur, propiusque aestus incendia volvunt.
"ergo age, care pater! cervici imponere nostrae!
ipse subibo umeris; nec me labor iste gravabit.
quo res cunque cadent, unum et commune periclum,

425 una salus ambobus erit. mihi parvus Iulus
sit comes, et longe servet vestigia coniunx.

427 **quae dicam:** Supply **ea** – *what I shall say.* **animis advertite:** The normal phrase is **animum advertite** with the dative case or **ad** plus the accusative, i.e. *turn your mind to.* In this line, the accusative and dative are reversed.

428 **est urbe egressis:** literally *there is to those who have left the city*, i.e. *as one leaves the city, there is. . . .*

429 **desertae:** *lonely.* The temples of Ceres, the Goddess of Crops and Agriculture, were usually built in secluded places so that they would be likely to be visited only by those who came to worship her.

430 **religione:** Not *by the religion*, but *by the religious observance.* Not unnaturally, people tended to regard very old trees with a certain awe, since both their size and their age seemed to suggest that there must be some supernatural power involved.

431 **ex diverso:** *from different directions, by different routes.*

432 **sacra:** Compare line 175.

433 **digressum** agrees with **me.**

434 **attrectare nefas:** Supply **est.** The ancients believed that those who had shed blood were unclean until they had washed their hands in running water. **vivo:** *running*; it seemed alive because it was moving.

435 **abluero:** an unfinished line. Compare line 46.

436 **haec fatus:** Compare line 38 (LN # 39). **latos umeros insternor:** another example of the passive voice being used to imitate the Greek Middle Voice. **insternor** is literally *I cover myself*; this reflexive use is then extended to take a direct object in the sense *I put on* or *I cover.* (Cf. lines 107, 158, 233 and 243.) (LN # 20) **subiecta:** literally *placed under*, i.e. to lift his father. It is best to translate this as a main verb – *I stooped* or *I bent down.* The timing of the tenses is not quite accurate. Presumably, he would put on the lion-skin and then stoop to lift his father. (Hysteron Proteron: LN # 35)

437 **super** is used adverbially – *on top.* **fulvique:** an example of -que being used in an explanatory sense rather than with its usual meaning *and.* The phrase **fulvi pelle leonis** explains what the **veste** was; translate *consisting of* or *namely* (LN # 37).

438 **dextrae se implicuit:** literally *entwined himself to my right hand*, i.e. *slipped his hand into my right hand* (or simply *into mine*); a lovely touch of tenderness.

439 **non passibus aequis:** The short legs of Iulus had to work overtime to keep up with his father striding along.

vos, famuli, quae dicam, animis advertite vestris.
est urbe egressis tumulus templumque vetustum
desertae Cereris, iuxtaque antiqua cupressus,
430 religione patrum multos servata per annos.
hanc ex diverso sedem veniemus in unam.
tu, genitor, cape sacra manu patriosque Penates!
me, bello e tanto digressum et caede recenti,
attrectare nefas, donec me flumine vivo
435 abluero."
haec fatus, latos umeros subiectaque colla
veste super fulvique insternor pelle leonis;
succedoque oneri.   dextrae se parvus Iulus
implicuit, sequiturque patrem non passibus aequis.
440 pone subit coniunx.   ferimur per opaca locorum.
et me, quem dudum non ulla iniecta movebant
tela neque adverso glomerati ex agmine Grai,

---

440 **ferimur per opaca locorum:** For this use of **fero** (*we made our way*)
compare line 384. The use of the genitive **locorum** gives a slightly
different meaning from **opaca loca:** wherever they were, they picked
the *shady (parts) of the places* rather than *they went through shady
places*.

441 **non ulla tela = nulla tela.   movebant:** *moved* in the sense *made an
impression* or *worried*, i.e. he didn't turn a hair.

442 **adverso ex agmine:** We would probably translate (*massed*) **in** *their
hostile ranks*; the **ex** does add something to the scene, however, in
that it suggests both the hurling of weapons from their ranks and
the charges which they would make from time to time into the ranks
of the Trojans.

443 **omnes aurae:** *every breath of air.* **terrent:** The object of this verb is **me** in line 441. This is a common human experience; men and women who have shown not the slightest trace of fear when in the midst of terrible danger can become very apprehensive when faced with uncertainty. Waiting for something to happen can be more frightening than the danger itself.

444 **suspensum** and **timentem** both agree with **me** in line 441.
comitique onerique: -que. . . -que . . . . means *both . . . . and.* His companion was, of course, Iulus and his burden was his father.

446 **evasisse viam:** Normally **evadere** would not take an object. Here the road is regarded as a danger that he has escaped. Translate *to have completed my journey in safety.* **creber** agrees with **sonitus** in the next line. The literal meaning of **creber** is *thick.* The word is used here because many people are hurrying along, all out of step, so that the sounds are packed together. Translate *the sound of many feet.*

447 **visus:** Supply **est.**

446–7 The rhythm of these lines conveys the sound of the rapid tramping of feet.

448 **propinquant:** *they* refers to the enemy.

450 **nescio quod numen:** *some power or other.* The phrase **nescio quod** is really a kind of parenthesis which is then used adjectivally (literally *a power, I know not which power. . .*). The expression explains very well how puzzled Aeneas is that he should even have contemplated such a silly thing. **male amicum:** For this use of **male** as a very strong negative compare line 12; *not friendly* = *hostile.* **trepido:** dative agreeing with **mihi** – *from me in my alarm.* The dative depends on **eripuit** (the person from whom something is snatched).

451 **avia cursu sequor:** literally *I followed pathless places in my running,* i.e. *I ran along side-streets.*

452 **nota excedo regione viarum:** *I departed from the well-known direction of the streets,* i.e. *I left the route which I knew through the streets.* **regio** may mean *region* but, since he was trying to reach a destination, it is more likely that it has its original meaning here; *direction* is derived from the verb **regere** which means literally *to direct.*

453 **misero:** Supply **mihi.** For the dative with **eripere**, see line 450. **fatone:** The interrogative suffix **-ne** would normally be attached to the first word in the question. The poet is allowed this freedom to suit his metre. Note that the 'while' clause is followed, rather unusually, by a question instead of a statement, thus illustrating Virgil's artistry in describing Aeneas' confused state of mind – one train of thought changing rapidly to another.

nunc omnes terrent aurae, sonus excitat omnis
suspensum et pariter comitique onerique timentem.
445 iamque propinquabam portis, omnemque videbar
evasisse viam, subito cum creber ad aures
visus adesse pedum sonitus, genitorque per umbram
prospiciens "nate," exclamat "fuge, nate! propinquant.
ardentes clipeos atque aera micantia cerno."

31 Panic and disaster

In panic, I decided to take a different route to protect my
companions and lost my way. When I finally reached the
rendezvous, Creusa was missing.

450 hic mihi nescio quod trepido male numen amicum
confusam eripuit mentem. namque avia cursu
dum sequor, et nota excedo regione viarum,
heu! misero coniunx fatone erepta Creusa
substitit? erravitne via seu lassa resedit?
455 incertum; nec post oculis est reddita nostris.
nec prius amissam respexi animumve reflexi

---

454 **via** = **a via**. By scanning the line we discover that the -a of **via** is
long, making it ablative. What about **lassa**? Is the final -**a** long or
short? What does it agree with? **seu:** *or.*

455 **incertum:** Supply **est.** **post** is used adverbially.

456 **nec prius . . . respexi . . . quam:** *I did not look back until.* For this
split use of **priusquam** meaning *until* after a negative word compare
AIC 101. Note that **prius** is not translated till the place where **quam**
appears. (Tmesis: LN # 28) **amissam:** Supply **uxorem** or **coniu-
gem** or **Creusam.** He did not, of course, know at the time that she
was lost. Translate *my lost one.*

457 **tumulum sedemque:** accusative of motion without preposition (LN # 1). **sedemque:** another example of explanatory **-que** (LN # 37). **tumulum** and **sedem** refer to the same spot, but each word looks at a different aspect of the place.

458 **hic demum: demum** emphasises **hic** – *here and only here* did they actually realise that Creusa was missing.

459 **fefellit:** literally *deceived*; i.e. she promised she would meet them there and did not appear. Translate *failed to meet.*

460 **hominum:** genitive with **quem.** Note that the final vowel of **deorumque** is elided before the vowel at the beginning of the next line.

464 **cingor:** The passive is used reflexively but, unlike lines 158, 233 and 243, it is not used like the Greek Middle Voice to govern a direct object (LN # 20). At first sight, it seems strange to mention **urbem peto** before **cingor armis,** but probably the former suggests his decision to go back, which would then put the actions in the correct order.

466 **qua:** The relative refers back to **portae. gressum extuleram:** a poetic way of saying *I had left* (*the city*). **vestigia retro observata sequor: retro sequor** means *I retraced.* The participle **observata** is awkward to translate although it is easy to see what is meant: in retracing his steps he worked out the route he had taken by noting landmarks as he went along. Translate *I retraced my steps, recalling as I went the route I had taken.*

467 **lumine:** *with my eyes* – poetic singular for plural (LN # 3)

468 **animos:** poetic plural.
terrent has two subjects: **horror** and **silentia.**

469 **pedem tulisset:** Compare line 466 for this poetic way of saying *she had gone.* **si forte . . . tulisset:** The use of the subjunctive shows that these are his thoughts expressed in indirect speech. His direct thoughts would have been *I shall go home to see if she has gone there.* The repetition of **si forte** expresses his feeling that there was just the slimmest chance that she *might* have gone home.

472 **exsuperant:** For the basic meaning of this word compare lines 108, 178 and 380. Note how the short sentences in this line and the next convey the idea of his frantic search.

473 **sedes:** poetic plural.

474 **porticibus**: Supply **in. Iunonis asylo:** *under the protection of Juno.* Normally, a temple would have been a place of sanctuary for someone trying to escape an enemy. The irony of the situation was that Juno, who favoured the Greeks, was giving her protection to booty which the Greeks were storing there.

475 **Phoenix** had been a comrade of Achilles.

quam tumulum antiquae Cereris sedemque sacratam
venimus: hic demum collectis omnibus una
defuit, et comites natumque virumque fefellit.
460 quem non incusavi amens hominumque deorumque?
aut quid in eversa vidi crudelius urbe?

32 Frantic search

I went back on my own to look for Creusa. The Greeks
were looting and burning everywhere, and soldiers were
standing guard over the plunder and the captive women and
children.

Ascanium Anchisenque patrem Teucrosque Penates
commendo sociis, et curva valle recondo;
ipse urbem repeto, et cingor fulgentibus armis.
465 principio muros obscuraque limina portae,
qua gressum extuleram, repeto; et vestigia retro
observata sequor per noctem et lumine lustro.
horror ubique animos, simul ipsa silentia terrent.
inde domum, si forte pedem, si forte, tulisset,
470 me refero. inruerant Danai, et tectum omne tenebant.
ilicet ignis edax summa ad fastigia vento
volvitur; exsuperant flammae; furit aestus ad auras.
procedo, et Priami sedes arcemque reviso.
et iam porticibus vacuis Iunonis asylo
475 custodes lecti Phoenix et dirus Ulixes

476 **Troia** has three syllables, showing that it is from the adjective **Troius**. The noun **Troia** has only two syllables.

478 **auro solidi**: literally *solid with gold*, i.e. *of solid gold*. **vestis**: Singular for plural. Cf. line 467 (LN # 3).

479 **congeritur** is singular agreeing with the nearest subject **vestis**, although it is the verb for all the subjects in the sentence.

480 This is another unfinished line, in this case possibly intentionally so in order to increase the dramatic horror of what he saw.

481 **quin etiam** is a very strong *even*, i.e. incredible though it may seem. **voces**: poetic plural.

483 **iterumque iterumque**: These words in particular vividly portray his frantic search.

484 **quaerenti et . . . furenti**: These participles agree with **mihi** in line 486. Translate *as I searched frantically*. **tectis**: Again, an ablative of place without the preposition. Compare line 474.

486 **visa**: Supply **est**. It agrees with **umbra**, although it is also the verb for **simulacrum** and **imago**. All three nouns refer to Creusa's ghost. **nota maior imago**: By scanning the line, we discover that the **-a** of **nota** is long, making it ablative, i.e. Ablative of Comparison with **Creusa** understood. Literally it means *an image larger than known*. Translate *a figure larger than the Creusa he knew*. The ghosts of the dead, like the gods themselves, were believed to be larger than living human beings.

487 **obstipui**: Note the very strong pause in the second foot, used to produce dramatic effect. **steterunt**: Note how Virgil has allowed himself to shorten the second **e** for metrical reasons.

488 **adfari** is a historic infinitive (cf. lines 70 and 404). Translate *she began to speak to me*. **demere** is also a historic infinitive (LN # 23).

489 **quid**: *why*?

490 **non sine numine divom**: The double negative *not without* makes this a very positive statement: *it is definitely by divine will* that this has happened.

491 **comitem**: used predicatively *as a companion* (LN # 36).

492 **nec fas aut ille regnator**: Both the impersonal verb **fas est** (*it is allowed*) and the personal verb **sinit** (subject **regnator**) govern **te asportare**. Translate *neither divine law nor that ruler . . ..* The divine law had to be obeyed even by the gods themselves. **regnator Olympi** refers to Jupiter (Zeus).

493 **tibi**: *by you* – dative of agent, as is normal with Gerundive of Obligation (LN # 7). **exsilia**: poetic plural. Since **arandum (est)** makes sense only with **aequor**, another gerundive (e.g. **patienda sunt**) must be understood with **exsilia**.

praedam adservabant. huc undique Troia gaza
incensis erepta adytis mensaeque deorum
crateresque auro solidi captivaque vestis
congeritur. pueri et pavidae longo ordine matres
480 stant circum.

33 Creusa bids farewell

Again and again, I called my wife's name as I ran through
the streets. Suddenly her ghost appeared and told me not
to worry over her; at least she would not be carried off into
slavery.

ausus quin etiam voces iactare per umbram
implevi clamore vias, maestusque Creusam
nequiquam ingeminans iterumque iterumque vocavi.
quaerenti et tectis urbis sine fine furenti
485 infelix simulacrum atque ipsius umbra Creusae
visa mihi ante oculos, et nota maior imago.
obstipui, steteruntque comae, et vox faucibus haesit.
tum sic adfari et curas his demere dictis:
"quid tantum insano iuvat indulgere dolori,
490 o dulcis coniunx? non haec sine numine divom
eveniunt; nec te hinc comitem asportare Creusam
fas aut ille sinit superi regnator Olympi.
longa tibi exsilia, et vastum maris aequor arandum;
et terram Hesperiam venies, ubi Lydius arva
495 inter opima virum leni fluit agmine Thybris.

---

494 **terram Hesperiam**: literally *the land in the west*, i.e. Italy. For the
omission of the preposition see LN # 1. **Lydius Thybris**: The Tiber
is called *Lydian* since, according to legend, the Etruscans, who
inhabited the land on the north side of the Tiber, came originally
as colonists from Lydia in Asia Minor.

495 **virum = virorum**. Although genitive, it is best translated as *worked
by husbandmen*. **leni agmine**: *with slow current, gently.*

496 **res laetae:** *prosperity*. Note the alliteration based on the letter **r** (LN # 33).

497 **parta tibi:** Supply **est** – *have been won for you, are waiting for you*. The verb agrees with the nearest subject **coniunx**, but has also as its subjects **res** and **regnum**.   **regia coniunx:** Aeneas was to marry Lavinia, the daughter of King Latinus.   **lacrimas Creusae:** not *the tears* **of** *Creusa*, but *the tears* **for** *Creusa*. (Objective genitive: LN # 6)

498 **Myrmidonum, Dolopum, Grais:** different names for the Greeks.

499 **servitum** is the supine of **servire** and is used after a verb of motion to denote purpose: *to be a slave*. Her death had saved her from such a fate.

500 **magna deum genetrix:** This was Cybele, who is often identified with the earth, which is the mother of all things. She was especially worshipped in Phrygia and on Mount Ida, and so was favourable to the Trojans.

501 **nati communis:** *of the son who belongs to us both*.

502 **lacrimantem et volentem:** Supply **me**.

504 **conatus:** Supply **sum**.   **ibi:** *there and then*.   **dare . . . circum: circum** is not a preposition but part of the verb **circumdare** which has been split up and inverted. (Cf. lines 107 and 456 for other examples of Tmesis: LN # 28.)   **collo** is dative: *round her neck*. **ter:** There was a strong religious significance in the number 3.

505 **frustra:** Take with **comprensa**. It was futile to try to embrace her because she was a ghost.   **manus:** accusative plural.

506 **volucrique: -que** here means *or*.

507 **sic:** Take with **consumpta nocte:** he spent the night searching for her and only gave up when daylight was approaching.

509 **admirans:** *to my surprise*; or *I was surprised to find*.

510 **exsilio:** Dative of Purpose *for exile* (LN # 8). Take with **collectam**. **pubem:** Certainly not *young men* here; it may simply mean *people*, or possibly *young people* contrasting with older generation **matresque virosque.**

511 **animis opibusque parati:** *ready in spirit and with their possessions*. Some idea such as *to follow me* or *to go* is needed to link this with the next line. The passage reminds us of the pathetic picture of refugees in the modern world.

512 **velim** is subjunctive because it expresses their thoughts in indirect speech. They said to themselves *we are ready to go wherever you wish to lead us*.   **pelago:** ablative meaning literally *by sea* (cf. **terra marique**). Translate *across the sea*.   **deducere** is the technical word used for taking people across the sea to found a colony.

illic res laetae regnumque et regia coniunx
parta tibi. lacrimas dilectae pelle Creusae.
non ego Myrmidonum sedes Dolopumve superbas
aspiciam, aut Grais servitum matribus ibo.
500 sed me magna deum genetrix his detinet oris.
iamque vale! et nati serva communis amorem!"
haec ubi dicta dedit, lacrimantem et multa volentem
dicere deseruit, tenuesque recessit in auras.
ter conatus ibi collo dare bracchia circum;
505 ter frustra comprensa manus effugit imago,
par levibus ventis, volucrique simillima somno.
sic demum socios consumpta nocte reviso.

34 Departure

When I returned to the rendezvous, I found many others
there ready to flee with me into exile.

atque hic ingentem comitum adfluxisse novorum
invenio admirans numerum, matresque virosque,
510 collectam exsilio pubem, miserabile vulgus.
undique convenere, animis opibusque parati,
in quascunque velim pelago deducere terras.
iamque iugis summae surgebat Lucifer Idae,
ducebatque diem. Danaique obsessa tenebant
515 limina portarum, nec spes opis ulla dabatur:
cessi, et sublato montes genitore petivi.'

---

513 **Lucifer**: *the Morning Star* (derived from **lux** and **fero**).
iugis: literally *from the ridges*. We would more naturally say *over the ridges*.

515 **spes opis**: *hope of (bringing) help (to the city)*. Only then did he finally give in to the will of the gods. Note the powerful effect of the single word **cessi**, followed by the promise of hope for the future when he lifted his father on his shoulders and headed for the hills as a new day began to dawn.

·LANGUAGE NOTES·

Because of the difficulties involved in fitting words into the metre, the poet allows himself a certain freedom to vary the strict grammatical usages of Classical Latin. These have been explained in the notes as they occur, but the following summary should prove useful by bringing together various examples of the same usage.

AIC refers to lines in 'Arrival in Carthage.'
LDOT refers to lines in 'The Last Days of Troy.'

PREPOSITIONS

#1 *Prepositions are frequently omitted in poetry:*

(a) By far the most common is the omission of **in** with the ablative case, e.g. **celsa sedet Aeolus arce** (AIC 26)
Compare AIC 10, 22, 47, 53, 63, 121, 168, 207, 225, 245, 253, 272, 321, 332; LDOT 19, 22, 34, 76, 133, 229, 302, 474, 484.

(b) **ad** or **in** with the accusative case, e.g.
Aeoliam venit (AIC 22)
terram Hesperiam venies (LDOT 494)
Compare AIC 2 and LDOT 457.

(c) **ab**: e.g. **alto prospiciens** (AIC 61)
Compare AIC 294 and LDOT 454.

(d) **ex**: e.g.
caput extulit unda (AIC 62)
telis elapsus (LDOT 189)

(e) **sub**: e.g. **media testudine templi** (AIC 162)

(f) **trans**: e.g. **maria omnia vecti** (AIC 178)

NOUNS

#2 *Plural used instead of singular (Poetic Plural):*

e.g. **sceptra** for **sceptrum** (AIC 27).

This is very common in Virgil: AIC 9, 19, 29, 42, 48, 65, 143, 145, 146, 148, 182, 216, 227, 253, 266, 284, 286, 317, 321; LDOT 4, 11, 23, 65, 73,

95, 113, 120, 135, 164, 187, 231, 254, 271, 285, 307, 319, 320, 321, 350, 354, 361, 374, 379, 380, 421, 468, 473, 481, 493.

#3 *Singular for plural*: **armato milite complent** (LDOT 9) (cf. 308, 467, 478)

#4 *Greek accusatives* are commonly used for proper names; there are two forms:

(i) **Anthea**: AIC 90, 167   **Laocoonta**: LDOT 102, 118
   Ilionea: AIC 229   **aethera**: AIC 212; LDOT 202
   Sidona: AIC 237

(ii) **Capyn**: AIC 92   **Aenean**: AIC 206, 247
    Gyan: AIC 130, 230   **Achaten**: AIC 259
    Acesten: AIC 195   **Anchisen** (LDOT 462)

#5 *Contracted genitive*

Danaum for **Danaorum**: AIC 14, 330; LDOT 7, 25, 33, 64, 220, 239, 248, 286

divom for **divorum**: AIC 31, 248; LDOT 129, 154, 200, 329, 490

deum for **deorum**: LDOT 136, 500

superum for **superorum**: AIC 4

virum for **virorum**: AIC 45, 56; LDOT 184, 495

Teucrum for **Teucrorum**: LDOT 163

Achivom for **Achivorum**: LDOT 189

#6 *Objective genitive*

donum Minervae (LDOT 20) *gift presented to Minerva* (not *gift of Minerva*) (Cf. LDOT 82.)

lacrimas Creusae (LDOT 487): *tears shed for Creusa* (not *Creusa's tears*)

#7 *Dative of Agent*

Tros Tyriusque mihi agetur (AIC 199) (*by me*)

non umquam credita Teucris (LDOT 135) (*by the Trojans*)

tibi arandum (LDOT 493) (*by you*)

#8 *Other uses of the dative*

   multos demittimus Orco (LDOT 248) (Motion)

   glomerare manum bello (LDOT 186) (Purpose)

   auxilio subeuntem (LDOT 105) (Predicative)

   collo squamea terga circumdati (LDOT 107)

   collectam exsilio (LDOT 510) (Purpose)

   viro manicas vincla levari iubet (LDOT 57) (Ethic)

#9 *Accusative of Respect*

vultum demissa (AIC 190): *cast down as far as her face was concerned*, i.e. *lowering her eyes.*
animum arrecti (AIC 204): *raised up with respect to their spirit*, i.e. *cheered up.*
os umerosque deo similis (AIC 214): *like a god with respect to his face and shoulders*, i.e. *godlike in face and shoulders.*
faciem mutatus (AIC 273): *changed in appearance.*
expleri mentem (AIC 309): *to be satisfied in mind.*
manus revinctum (LDOT 41): *bound as to his hands*, i.e. *with his hands bound.*

#10 *Ablative of Respect*

bello maior (AIC 189): *greater in war.*
Compare: **iustior pietate** (AIC 189)

#11 *Ablative of Description*

tonsis mantelia villis (AIC 302)

#12 *Instrumental Ablative*

stridens Aquilone procella (AIC 48)
vento petiisse Mycenas (LDOT 14)

See also LDOT 26, 56, 80, 253

#13 *Ablative of Accompaniment*

magno misceri murmure (AIC 60)

ADJECTIVES

#14 *Transferred Epithet* (epithet = adjective)

molem hanc immanis equi (LDOT 61), where the notion of 'huge' goes more naturally with **molem.**
quae tam sera moratur segnities? (LDOT 223), where the idea of lateness is transferred to the cause of the lateness.
Compare LDOT 321.

#15 **summus, medius and imus**

Where English uses the *nouns* 'top', 'middle' and 'bottom' followed by 'of' and another noun, Latin uses the adjectives **summus, medius** and **imus** agreeing with the second noun:

mari summo	on the surface of the sea (AIC 53)
summa unda	from the top of the wave (AIC 62)
summo de vertice	from the top of his head (LDOT 401)

summa ad fastigia	to the top of the roof (LDOT 471)
mediis tectis	in the middle of the palace (AIC 253)
medios in hostes	into the midst of the enemy (LDOT 227)
medium in agmen	into the middle of the battle (LDOT 258)
aedibus in mediis	in the middle of the palace (LDOT 325)
in media morte	in the throes of death (LDOT 345)
imo de pectore	from the bottom of his heart (LDOT 170)
summae Idae	of the top of Ida (LDOT 513)

There are other occasions, of course, when these words are used as adjectives in the normal way, e.g.

imas fores	the lowest doors (the doors below) (LDOT 278)

#16 *Superlative attracted into relative clause*

collem qui plurimus urbi imminet (AIC 136)
vulnera gerens quae plurima accepit (LDOT 160)
Even in Latin prose, superlative adjectives are frequently attracted into the relative clause. English would tend to say 'the very big hill which . . .' and 'the very many wounds which . . .

VERBS

#17 *The ending* **-ere**

Two forms of the 3rd person plural of the perfect indicative active are used by Virgil: the normal prose ending **-erunt** and the less common **-ere** ending. The alternative forms give the poet more flexibility because of their different metrical quantities: ¯ ¯ and - ˘. The **-ere** form is very common, e.g.

AIC 5, 42, 48, 65, 224, 304.
LDOT 1, 40, 61, 68, 76, 78, 91, 131, 141, 164, 279, 318, 511.

#18 *Contracted forms*

repostum for **repositum** (AIC 10)
onerarat for **oneraverat** (AIC 104)
adflarat for **adflaverat** (AIC 216)
accestis for **accessistis** (AIC 109)
violasset for **violavisset** (LDOT 82)
foedasti for **foedavisti** (LDOT 350)
(Cf. LDOT 378.)

#19 *Omission of* **esse**

(i) as a verb in its own right:

AIC 37, 114, 319; LDOT 4, 12, 31, 33, 51, 111, 185, 193, 218, 252, 418, 434, 455, 493.

AIC 235 where **es** is omitted.

LDOT 19, 24 where **erat** is omitted.

LDOT 73, 221 where **esse** is omitted.

(ii) *from passive forms*

The most common is the omission of **est**, e.g. **exempta** for **exempta est** (AIC 124). Compare AIC 174, 241, 259; LDOT 2, 71, 89, 173, 355, 356, 370, 374, 401, 446, 486, 497.

Other forms are quite common:

e.g. **dicta** for **dicta sunt** (AIC 39). Compare AIC 174; LDOT 69, 71, 280

datum for **datum esse** (AIC 71). Compare LDOT 32, 84, 86, 120.

experti for **experti estis** (AIC 110)
conatus for **conatus sum** (LDOT 504)
rati for **rati sumus** (LDOT 14)
capti for **capti sumus** (LDOT 89)

#20 *Passive used reflexively*

Sometimes the Passive Voice is used to imitate the Greek Middle Voice, producing a reflexive meaning, e.g.

implentur (AIC 123) = **se implent**

Compare

teguntur (LDOT 115) = **se tegunt**
conduntur (LDOT 251) = **se condunt**
circumfundimur (LDOT 233) = **nos circumfundimus**
protecti (LDOT 276) = *protecting themselves*
cingi (LDOT 332), **cingor** (LDOT 464)

Sometimes this reflexive use of the passive is extended to govern a direct object, e.g.

exuvias indutus (LDOT 158), *having put on the spoils.*
(eos) circumfundimur (LDOT 233), *we surrounded them.*
galeam induitur (LDOT 243), *he put on his helmet.*
ferrum cingitur (LDOT 323), *he put on his sword.*

The most complicated example in the book can be found at LDOT 107 where a detailed explanation is given. (See also LDOT 422, 436.)

#21 *Continuous present in the past*

e.g. **iamdudum timemus**, *we have been afraid for a long time* (and are still afraid)

Compare AIC 106: **ante** is used with the present tense to indicate something which existed in the past and still continues — **neque enim ignari sumus ante malorum**, *we have not previously been* (*nor are we now*) *ignorant of misfortune.*

Compare the use of the present participle **volvens** in AIC 131 and the use of the imperfect in AIC 205:

iamdudum ardebant, *they had been* (*and still were*) *eager.*

#22 *Historic present*

The present tense is very common throughout the *Aeneid*. It is used to convey vividness. Translate into a past tense.

e.g. **vastos volvunt ad litora fluctus.**
They rolled huge breakers up on the shore.

#23 *Historic infinitive*

Occasionally, the infinitive is used instead of the indicative, e.g.
fluere and **referri** in LDOT 70. (Cf. 404, 488.)

#24 *Infinitive of purpose*

The infinitive can sometimes be used in poetry to convey purpose, e.g.
populare venimus (AIC 181), *we came to plunder.*

#25 **o** with a perfect participle

o passi graviora (AIC 107), O *(you who have) suffered.*
o sola miserata (AIC 220), O *(you who have) alone pitied.*

FIGURES OF SPEECH

#26 *Simile*

In Virgil the beginning of a simile is usually marked by a word such as **qualis, velut** or **ceu**, e.g.

velut agmine facto (AIC 40)	*just as if in formed ranks*
veluti cum . . . (LDOT 179)	*just as when . . .*
veluti qui . . . (LDOT 229)	*just like the man who . . .*
qualis . . . labor (AIC 146)	*just like the work. . .*
qualis . . . Diana (AIC 156)	*just like Diana*
qualis mugitus (LDOT 111)	*just like the bellowing*
atra ceu tempestate (LDOT 328)	*just as in a storm*
non sic (LDOT 309)	*even more violent*

Similes tend to be quite long in Virgil and so another word is used to mark the end of the simile. For example,

in line 232 of LDOT **haud secus** (*not otherwise*) concluding the simile which began with **veluti**.

Compare **talis erat Dido** which follows **qualis Diana** (AIC 160).

#27 *Hendiadys*

This means literally *one through two*, i.e. two expressions are used to convey one notion, e.g.

> **vinclis et carcere** (AIC 24), *by chains and prison*, i.e. *prison chains*.
> **signis auroque** (AIC 263), *with markings and gold*, i.e. *with gold embroidery*.
> **telis et luce coruscus aena** (LDOT 290), *glittering with weapons and bronze light*, i.e. *gleaming with the glint of his bronze armour*.
> **voci iraeque** (LDOT 346), *his voice and anger*, i.e. *his angry words*.

#28 *Tmesis*

In this figure of speech, the two parts of a compound are separated by another word, e.g.

> **circum nutrimenta dedit** (AIC 84) – the compound word being **circumdedit**
> **quae me cunque** (AIC 228) – where **me** intervenes in **quaecunque**
> **circum terga dati** (LDOT 107) – compare AIC 84
> **nec prius abstitit quam** (AIC 101) – compare LDOT 456
> **quo res cunque** (LDOT 424)
> **dare bracchia circum** (LDOT 504)

#29 *Zeugma*

In the following examples, the meaning of the verb goes naturally with one of the objects but not with the other, for which English would require to supply another verb:

> **Danaos et claustra laxat** (LDOT 144) – *He loosened the bolt and* **freed** *the Greeks.*
> **sacra victosque deos parvumque nepotem trahit** (LDOT 191) – *He* **carried** *sacred emblems and the conquered gods and dragged his little grandson.*

#30 *Metaphor*

Poetry is full of metaphors, i.e. words used in an unusual way to produce poetic images, e.g.

incendia miscet (LDOT 199)
placidam quietem inrigat (AIC 293)
fluere ac retro sublapsa referri spes (LDOT 70)
thalami . . . et postes . . . procubuere (LDOT 317)
quo res cunque cadent (LDOT 424)

#31 *Metonymy*

In the following examples, the name of a deity is substituted for something connected with the deity:

Cererem (AIC 86 and 301), where the name of the Goddess of Agriculture is substituted for *corn*.
Bacchi (AIC 123), where the God of Wine is used for *wine*.
foribus divae (AIC 162), where *the goddess* is used for *her temple*.

#32 *Synecdoche*

The part of something is used to signify the whole thing, or vice versa, e.g.

carinis (LDOT 12 and 76) where the keel of the ship is used for *ship*.

#33 *Alliteration*

This occurs when words containing the same sound or letter appear in close succession. It is very common in Latin poetry, sometimes used to convey meaning through the sound of the words (see also Onomatopoeia), and sometimes used for its own sake as part of the poet's armoury.

magno cum murmure montis (AIC 25)
circum claustra (AIC 26)
incute vim ventis (AIC 35)
cavum conversa cuspide montem (AIC 39)
vastos volvunt (AIC 44)
magno misceri murmure (AIC 60)
prospectum late pelago petit (AIC 90)
panduntur portae (LDOT 16)
validis ingentem viribus (LDOT 38)
fit sonitus spumante salo (LDOT 99)
res laetae regnumque et regia coniunx (LDOT 496)
(Cf. LDOT 211, 212, 217–8, 281, 381.)

117

#34 *Onomatopoeia*

In this figure of speech, the sound of the words suggests the object or action they describe. In the examples of alliteration, see especially the first example which depicts the whining and moaning of the winds, and the second last example which imitates the swishing sound of the waves. Other examples include:

> **insequitur clamorque virum stridorque rudentum** (AIC 45)
> **franguntur remi** (AIC 50)
> **insequitur cumulo praeruptus aquae mons** (AIC 51)
> hastam
> **contorsit. stetit illa tremens, uteroque recusso**
> **insonuere cavae gemitumque dedere cavernae.** (LDOT 38–40)

#35 *Hysteron Proteron*

This figure of speech occurs when the time sequence of two ideas is reversed, e.g.

> **submersas obrue** (AIC 35): *overwhelm and sink*
> **inclusos Danaos et claustra laxat** (LDOT 144) *he loosened the bolts and freed the Greeks inside.*
> Compare LDOT 436.

MISCELLANEOUS

#36 *Used predicatively*

This expression is used frequently in the notes. The following examples will illustrate what is meant:

> **Iuno supplex** (AIC 30) *Juno as a suppliant* (cf. AIC 278)
> **capita alta ferentes** (AIC 98) – *holding their heads high* (**not** *holding their high heads*)
> **premit altum corde dolorem** (AIC 117) – *he kept back his sorrow deep in his heart* (**not** *his deep sorrow*)
> **domus interior regali splendida luxu** (AIC 252), *the house splendid with . . .*
> **rapidum praemittit Achaten** (AIC 259) *sent Achates speeding*
> **insonuere cavae . . . cavernae** (LDOT 40), *the recesses sounded hollow*
> **haec edissere vera** (LDOT 60), *explain these things truthfully*
> **immensam attollere molem** (LDOT 79), *to make the body huge*
> **hos cape comites** (LDOT 176), *take these as companions*
> **praecipites trahit silvas** (LDOT 182), *dragged the woods headlong*
> **addunt se socios** (LDOT 203), *they added themselves as allies*
> **socia agmina credens** (LDOT 221), *believing the columns to be friendly*

invitis . . . fidere divis (LDOT 252), *to trust the gods if they are unwilling*

nuntius ibis (LDOT 358), *you will go as a messenger*

comitem asportare Creusam (LDOT 491), *to take Creusa as a companion*

(Cf. LDOT 320, 419.)

SOME USES OF et, -que, ac AND atque

Besides the usual meaning 'and' the above words can have other meanings.

#37 For example, **-que** in particular is often used in an *explanatory* sense, i.e. it adds something to what is said.

Italiam Lavinaque (AIC 2), *Italy, namely, the shores of Lavinium.*

imperio premit ac vinclis et carcere frenat (AIC 24). Here the words after **ac** explain how he keeps them in check.

Ilium victosque Penates (AIC 34) – Ilium is represented by the Penates

in brevia et syrtes (AIC 54)

vulgus et omnem turbam (AIC 99)

Hesperiam magnam Saturniaque arva (AIC 194)

sacra suosque penates (LDOT 175)

sternit sata laeta boumque labores (LDOT 181)

exiit, oppositasque . . . (LDOT 310)

veste fulvique pelle (LDOT 437)

tumulum sedemque sacratam (LDOT 457)

#38 **-que . . . -que** (for the more usual **et . . . et . . .**)

una Eurusque Notusque ruunt creberque . . . (AIC 43)

insequitur clamorque virum stridorque rudentum (AIC 45)

exoritur clamorque virum clangorque tubarum (LDOT 184)

perque vias . . . perque domos . . . (LDOT 214)

comitique onerique (LDOT 444)

#39 *Poetic narrative convention*

By tradition, an epic poem such as the *Aeneid* would be recited, not read silently. So that the audience might know when someone's actual words were about to be quoted the poet used certain conventions which acted as 'markers', e.g.

dehinc talia fatur (AIC 66)   **adfari his dictis** (LDOT 488)

talia reddit (LDOT 194)

In the same way, 'markers' were required to show that the direct speech had ended:

talia voce refert (AIC 116)
talibus insidiis (LDOT 88)
talibus dictis (LDOT 200)
sic fatus (LDOT 38, 241, 355)
dixerat (LDOT 63, 420)
dixit (LDOT 226)
haec fatus (LDOT 436)
talia perstabat memorans (LDOT 383)
(Cf. LDOT 194, 338, 361, 398, 411, 502.)

#40 *Poetic expressions*

ab alto (AIC 53), *from the sea*
imbrem (AIC 59), *sea water*
ascensu supero (LDOT 178), *I climbed up*
cursu tendit (LDOT 192), *he was running*
religiosa deorum limina (LDOT 215), *hallowed portals of the gods*
(sacred temples)
clipei insigne decorum (LDOT 242), *the shield with its beautiful markings*
cursu petunt (LDOT 249), *they ran towards*
cursu sequor (LDOT 451), *I ran after*
gressum extuleram (LDOT 466), *I had left*
pedem tulisset (LDOT 469), *she had gone*
lapsu effugiunt (LDOT 113), *they glided away*

·COMPARISON WITH FULL TEXT·

I. "Arrival in Carthage" is all taken from Book 1:

Section
1. lines 1–4, 12, 15, 19–20, 25–33
2. lines 34–36, 51–59, 64–70
3. lines 76–77, 81–89
4. lines 90/102–105, 108, 110, 111, 118–120, 122–123
5. lines 124/5–134, 137–141
6. lines 142–143, 157–158, 170–179
7. lines 180–193
8. lines 194–195, 197–207
9. lines 208–222

10. lines 305–307,
    309/312–313, 419–425,
    427–433, 436–438
11. lines 495–501,
    503–504
12. lines 505–516
13. lines 520–528,
    530–531, 534–535,
    538, 544–545
14. lines 561–562,
    565–566, 569–578
15. lines 579–591,
    594–597, 603–612
16. lines 613–624,
    627–630
17. lines 631–635,
    637–642
18. lines 643–650,
    652–656
19. lines 657–660,
    663–664, 666, 677–696
20. lines 699–702,
    707–722
21. lines 723–725/740–741,
    747–756

II. "The Last Days of Troy" is all taken from Book 2:

Section
1. 1–3, 10, 12–13
2. 13–15, 20–24
3. 25–39
4. 40–46, 48–50, 52–53
5. 57–58, 63–72, 105–107
6. 108–144
7. 145–151
8. 152, 162–164, 166–171
9. 176–179, 183–187,
   189–198
10. 199–205, 209,
    211–220, 222–227
11. 228–249
12. 250–255
13. 258–261, 263–267
14. 268–271, 274–275,
    277–294
15. 302–308, 313–317
16. 318–326/327–329,
    336–338
17. 339–344, 359–369
18. 370–385
19. 386–401
20. 402–415, 424,
    426/427–430
21. 437–438/440–445,
    449–452,
    458–460/464–468
22. 469–470, 476–480,
    483–505
23. 506–513, 515–532
24. 533–535, 537–546
25. 547–553
26. 559–563, 624–625,
    632–633
27. 634–637, 641–643,
    645–646, 650
28. 655–656, 659, 668–684
29. 685–694, 699–704
30. 705–734
31. 735–746
32. 747–749, 752–767
33. 768–786, 788–795
34. 796–804

121

·THE GREEKS AND TROJANS·

The Greeks

Achivi
Argivi
Danai
Dolopes
Grai
Myrmidones
Pelasgi

The Trojans

Aeneadae
Dardanidae
Phryges
Teucri
Troes
Troiani

Adjectives

Argolicus
Doricus
Pelopeus

Iliacus
Phrygius
Troianus

Troy

Dardania
Ilium
Pergama (*n.pl*)
Troia

·VOCABULARY·

N.B. Where verbs are regular, they are listed without principal parts, e.g.
abnego (1), **moneo** (2) and **audio** (4).

A

a, ab (+ *abl.*), by, from
a tergo, behind
abdo, -ere, -didi, -ditum, to hide
abeo, -ire, -ii, -itum, to go away
abluo, -ere, -ui, -utum, to wash away
abnego (1), to refuse
aboleo, -ere, -evi, -itum, to abolish,
  efface, blot out the memory (of)
abripio, -ere, -ripui, -reptum, to snatch
absisto, -ere, -stiti, to stop, cease
abstineo, -ere, -ui, -tentum, to refrain,
  hold back
absum, -esse, afui, to be absent
ac, and
acanthus, -i (*m*), acanthus (plant)
accedo, -ere, -cessi, -cessum, to
  approach
accendo, -ere, -di, -censum, to set fire
  to
accingo, -ere, -nxi, -nctum, to make
  ready
  se accingere, to arm oneself
  ferro accingor, I gird myself with my
  sword
accipio, -ere, -cepi, -ceptum, to receive,
  learn, welcome
accitus, -us (*m*), summons, call
accommodo (1), to fit, hang on
acer, acris, acre, fierce
Acestes, -ae (*m*), Acestes (a Sicilian
  king)
Achates, -ae (*m*), Achates (the armour-
  bearer of Aeneas)
Achilles, -is or **-i** (*m*), Achilles (son of
  Peleus and Thetis)
Achivi, -orum (*m.pl*), the Greeks
Acidalia, -ae (*f*), Venus
acies, -ei (*f*), (line of) battle
ad (+ *acc.*), to, towards, near, at
addo, -ere, addidi, additum, to add
adflo (1), to breath upon
adfluo, -ere, -fluxi, -fluxum, to flow
  together
adfor, -fari, -fatus sum, to speak to,
  address
adforet = adesset

adglomero (1), to add
aditus, -us (*m*), entrance, approach
adloquor, -i, -locutus sum, to speak to
admiror (1), to wonder, be surprised at
adoro (1), to pray to
adno (1) to swim to, approach
adservo (1), to keep watch over
adspiro (1) (+ *dat.*), to breathe upon,
  be favourable to
adsto, -are, -stiti, to stand, stand by
adsum, -esse, adfui, to be present
adsurgo, -ere, -surrexi, -surrectum, to
  rise up
adultus, -a, -um, grown up
adversus, -a, -um, opposite, face on
adverto, -ere, -ti, -versum, to turn to
adytum, -i (*n*), shrine
aedes, -ium (*f.pl*), halls
aedifico (1), to build
aeger, -gra, -grum, sick, weary
Aeneadae, -um (*m.pl*), descendants of
  Aeneas, Trojans
Aeneas, -ae (*m*) (*acc.*, **Aenean**), Aeneas
  (son of Venus and Anchises)
aenum, -i (*n*), bronze vessel
aenus, -a, -um, made of bronze
Aeolus, -i (*m*), Aeolus (god of the
  winds)
aequaevus, -a, -um, of the same age
aequo (1), to make equal
aequor, -oris (*n*), level surface, sea
aequus, -a, -um, equal
aes, aeris (*n*), bronze
aestas, -atis (*f*), summer
aestus, -us (*m*), heat, hot blast
aeternus, -a, -um, everlasting
aether, -eris (*m*) (*acc.* **aethera**), air, sky
aevum, -i (*n*), age
Africus, -i (*m*), the South-West Wind
ager, agri (*m*), field
agger, -eris (*m*), bank
agitator, -oris (*m*), driver
agito (1), to pursue
agmen, -inis (*n*), line, course, stream,
  troop, column (of soldiers)
agnus, -i (*m*), lamb

ago, -ere, egi, actum, to drive, treat
age! agite!, come!
Aiax, Aiacis (*m*), Ajax (Greek hero)
aio (ait, aiunt), I say (he says, they say)
ala, -ae (*f*), wing
aliger, -era, -erum, winged
aliquis, -quid, someone, something
alius, alia, aliud, other, another
alii, -orum (*m.pl*), some, others
almus, -a, -um, kindly
altaria, -ium (*n. pl*), altar
alte, on high
alter, -era, -erum, another
altus, -a, -um, high, deep
  altum, -i (*n*) (or *pl*), the deep, the sea
alvus, -i (*f*), belly
amaracus, -i (*m*), marjoram (a sweet-smelling plant)
ambo, -bae, -bo, both
amens, -ntis, out of one's mind, mad
amictus, -a, -um, shrouded
amicus, -a, -um, friendly
amitto, -ere, -misi, -missum, to lose
amnis, -is (*m*), river
amor, -oris (*m*), love, desire
Amor, -oris (*m*), Cupid (the god of love)
amplector, -i, -plexus sum, to embrace, entwine
amplius, more
an, or
Anchises, -ae (*m*), Anchises (father of Aeneas)
Androgeos, -i (*m*), Androgeos (a Greek)
anguis, -is (*m*), snake
animus, -i (*m*), mind, spirit, heart
annus, -i (*m*), year
ante (*adv.*), previously
ante (+ *acc.*), before, in front of
antiquus, -a, -um, ancient
antrum, -i (*n*), cave
aperio, -ire, -ui, apertum, to open
apertus, -a, -um, open
apes, apis (*f*), bee
apex, apicis (*m*), point (of a flame)
Apollo, Apollinis (*m*), Apollo (god of divination and light)
appareo (2), to appear
applico (1), to drive, bring to
apto (1), to fit
apud (+ *acc.*), among
aqua, -ae (*f*), water
Aquilo, -onis (*m*), the North Wind
ara, -ae (*f*), altar

arboreus, -a, -um, tree-like, branching
arceo (2), to keep away, confine
arcus, -us (*m*), bow
ardens, -ntis, burning, excited, eager, flashing
ardeo, -ere, arsi, arsum, to be eager, burn
ardesco, -ere, arsi, to take fire, be enflamed
arduus, -a, -um, towering
argentum, -i (*n*), silver, silver-ware, silver-plate
Argi, -orum (*m.pl*), Argos (a town in the Peloponnese)
Argivus, -a, -um, Argive, Greek
Argolicus, -a, -um, Argolic, Greek
aridus, -a, -um, dry, parched
aries, -etis (*m*), battering-ram
arma, -orum (*n.pl*), arms, weapons, utensils
armatus, -a, -um, armed
  armati, -orum (*m.pl*), armed men
armentum, -i (*n*), beast, herd
armiger, -eri (*m*), armour-bearer
armo (1), to arm
aro (1), to plough
arrectus, -a, -um, encouraged
arrigo, -ere, -rexi, -rectum, to raise up, rear, prick up (ears)
ars, artis (*f*), art, skill, cunning, trick
artus, -a, -um, narrow, tight
artus, -us (*m*), limb
arvum, -i (*n*), field
arx, arcis (*f*), citadel, stronghold, defence-position
Ascanius, -i (*m*), Ascanius (son of Aeneas; also called Iulus)
ascendo, -ere, -di, -nsum, to climb
ascensus, -us (*m*), ascent
aspecto (1), to look at (towards)
aspectus, -us (*m*), sight
asper, -era, -erum, rough
aspicio, -ere, -spexi, -spectum, to behold, look upon
asporto (1), to carry away
ast, but
asylum, -i (*n*), place of refuge
at, but, on the other hand
ater, atra, atrum, black
Atlas, Atlantis (*m*), Atlas
atque, and
Atrides, -ae (*m*), son of Atreus
  Atridae, -arum (*m.pl*), Menelaus and Agamemnon
atrium, -i (*n*), hall, room
attollo, -ere, to raise up

attrecto (1), to touch, handle
auctor, -oris (*m*), author, inventor
audeo, -ere, ausus sum, to dare
audio (4), to hear
augurium, -i (*n*), omen
aula, -ae (*f*), hall
aura, -ae (*f*), air
  ad auras, to the sky
auratus, -a, -um, adorned with gold
aureus, -a, -um, golden
auris, -is (*f*), ear
Aurora, -ae (*f*), Aurora (goddess of the dawn)
aurum, -i (*n*), gold
Auster, Austri (*m*), the South Wind (a dry wind)
ausum, -i (*n*), a daring deed
aut, or
  aut . . . aut . . ., either . . . or . . .
autem, however
Automedon, -ontis (*m*), Automedon (charioteer of Achilles)
auxilium, -i (*n*), help
aveho, -ere, -vexi, -vectum, to carry off; (passive) to sail away
averto, -ere, -verti, -versum, to turn away
avidus, -a, -um, keen, eager
avius, -a, -um, pathless
  avia, -orum (*n.pl*), pathless wastes, places where there was no proper path
axis, -is (*m*), wheel, axis (of the earth), expanse, vault

B
bacatus, -a, -um, adorned with pearls
Bacchus, -i (*m*), Bacchus (god of wine)
barba, -ae (*f*), beard
barbaricus, -a, -um, barbarian, foreign, eastern
bellum, -i (*n*), war
bibo, -ere, bibi, to drink
bini, -ae, -a, two each, two, a pair
bipennis, -is (*f*), double-axe
biremis, -is (*f*), a bireme (ship with two banks of oars)
bis, twice
bonus, -a, -um, good
bos, bovis (*m*), ox
bracchium, -i (*n*), arm
brevia, -ium (*n. pl*), shallows
breviter, briefly

C
cadus, -i (*m*), cask

cado, -ere, cecidi, casum, to fall
caecus, -a, -um, blind, dark
caedes, -is (*f*), slaughter
caedo, -ere, cecidi, caesum, to kill, cut down
caelatus, -a, -um, engraved
caelicola, -ae (*m*), one who dwells in heaven
caelum, -i (*n*), heaven, sky
caerulus, -a, -um, dark blue
caesaries, -ei (*f*), a dark head of hair
Calchas, Calchantis (*m*), Calchas (a Greek prophet)
campus, -i (*m*), plain
canistrum, -i (*n*), basket
cano, -ere, cecini, cantum, to sing, sing of
capesso, -ere, -ivi, -itum, to undertake
capio, -ere, cepi, captum, to take, capture, trick
captus, -i (*m*), prisoner
captivus, -i (*m*), captive, plundered
capulus, -i (*m*), handle, hilt (of sword)
  capulo tenus, up to the hilt
caput, -itis (*n*), head
Capys, Capyos (*m*), Capys (companion of Aeneas)
carcer, -eris (*m*), prison
cardo, -inis (*m*), hinge, socket
careo (2) (+ *abl.*), to be without, lack
carina, -ae (*f*), keel, ship
carus, -a, -um, dear, loved, loving
Cassandra, -ae (*f*), Cassandra (daughter of Priam)
castra, -orum (*n.pl*), camp
casus, -us (*m*), fate, fall, misfortune
caterva, -ae (*f*), crowd
causa, -ae (*f*), reason
caverna, -ae (*f*), hollow, cavity
cavus, -a, -um, hollow
cedo, -ere, cessi, cessum, to go away, yield
celer, -eris, -ere, swift
celero (1), to do swiftly, speed
cella, -ae (*f*), cell
celsus, -a, -um, high, lofty
centum, hundred
cerealis, -is, -e, cooking, grinding
Ceres, Cereris (*f*), Ceres (goddess of crops); corn, bread
cerno, -ere, crevi, cretum, to see
certo (1), to fight, contend, vie with
certus, -a, -um, trustworthy, sure, unswerving
cervix, -icis (*f*), neck
cervus, -i (*m*), stag

cesso (1), to cease
ceteri, -ae, -a, the rest, the others
ceu, just like
chorus, -i (*m*), band of dancers
cingor, cingi, cinctus sum, to put on
circum (*adv.*), round about
circum (+ *acc.*), around
circumdo, -dare, -dedi, -datum, to put round
circumfundo, -ere, -fudi, -fusum, to surround
    circumfusus, -a, -um, surrounding, encircling
circumspicio, -ere, -spexi, -spectum, to look round
circumsto, -are, -steti, to stand round, surround
circumtextus, -a, -um, fringed
circumvolo (1), to fly round
cithara, -ae (*f*), lyre
cito, quickly
civis, -is (*m*), citizen
clades, -is (*f*), defeat, disaster, distress
clamor, -oris (*m*), shout, shouting
clangor, -oris (*m*), blaring (of trumpets)
clarus, -a, -um, clear
classis, -is (*f*), fleet
claustrum, -i (*n*), bar (for a door)
clipeus, -i (*m*), shield
coepi, coeptum, I have begun
cognomen, -inis (*n*), name, surname
cognosco, -ere, -novi, -nitum, to get to know
    cognitus, -a, -um, known
cogo, -ere, coegi, coactum, to force, compel
    coactus, -a, -um, forced, false
colligo, -ere, -legi, -lectum, to gather
collis, -is (*m*), hill
collum, -i (*n*), neck
colo, -ere, colui, cultum, to cultivate, cherish
colonus, -i (*m*), colonist
columba, -ae (*f*), dove
columna, -ae (*f*), pillar
coma, -ae (*f*), hair
comans, -ntis, hairy, crested
comes, -itis (*m*), companion
comitatus, -a, -um, accompanied
comitor (1), to accompany
commendo (1), to entrust
communis, -is, -e, common, shared
compages, -is (*f*), fastening
compello (1), to speak to, address
compello, -ere, -puli, -pulsum, to drive
complector, -i, -plexus sum, to embrace, enfold

compleo, -ere, -evi, -etum, to fill
complexus, -us (*m*), embrace
comprendo, -ere, -di, -nsum, to grasp
concedo, -ere, -cessi, -cessum, to withdraw
concido, -ere, -cidi, to fall down
conclamo (1), to shout together
concludo, -ere, -clusi, -clusum, to enclose
concretus, -a, -um, matted
concurro, -ere, -curri, -cursum, to run together
concursus, -us (*m*), gathering
condensus, -a, -um, packed together, huddled together
condo, -ere, condidi, -ditum, to found, hide
configo, -ere, -fixi, -fixum, to pierce through
confugio, -ere, -fugi, to flee to for refuge
confusus, -a, -um, confused, perplexed
congero, -ere, -gessi, -gestum, to heap together
congredior, -i, -gressus sum, to come together
conicio, -ere, -ieci, -iectum, to hurl
coniungo, -ere, -iunxi, -iunctum, to join
coniunx, -iugis (*f*), wife
conor (1), to try
conscendo, -ere, -ndi, -nsum, to climb
conscius, -a, -um, confederate, sharing knowledge with another
    sibi conscius, knowing something within oneself
consequor, -i, -secutus sum, to follow
consero, -ere, -serui, -sertum, to join, engage (in battle)
consido, -ere, -sedi, -sessum, to settle, sink down
consilium, -i (*n*), plan
consisto, -ere, -stiti, -stitum, to halt, stand still, settle, rest
conspectus, -us (*m*), sight, view
constituo, -ere, -ui, -utum, to decide
consumo, -ere, -sumpsi, -sumptum, to use up, spend
contendo, -ere, -ndi, -ntum, to hurry
conticesco, -ere, -ticui, to fall silent
contingo, -ere, -tigi, -tactum, to touch
contorqueo, -ere, -torsi, -tortum, to brandish, hurl
contra (*adv.*), in reply
contra (+ *acc.*), against
contrarius, -a, -um, opposing, contrary
convello, -ere, -velli, -vulsum, to tear down

convenio, -ire, -veni, -ventum, to come together

converto, -ere, -rti, -rsum, to turn

convexum, -i (*n*), vault, arch, hollow

convivium, -i (*n*), banquet

copia, -ae (*f*), opportunity

cor, cordis (*n*), heart

coram, face to face

cornu, -us (*n*), horn, antler

Coroebus, -i (*m*), Coroebus (son of Mygdon of Phrygia)

corona, -ae (*f*), crown

corono (1), to crown

corpus, -oris (*n*), body

corripio, -ere, -ripui, -reptum, to seize

corrumpo, -ere, -rupi, -ruptum, to spoil

coruscus, -a, -um, glittering, flashing

costa, -ae (*f*), rib

crater, -eris (*m*), (*acc. pl* **crateras**), bowl

creber, -bra, -brum, thick, frequent, abounding (in)

credo, -ere, -didi, -ditum (+ *dat.*), to believe, trust

Creusa, -ae (*f*), Creusa (wife of Aeneas)

crimen, -inis (*n*), crime, charge, accusation

crinis, -is (*m*), hair
  passis crinibus, with dishevelled hair

crinitus, -a, -um, long-haired

crispo (1), to swing, brandish

croceus, -a, -um, saffron, yellow

crudelis, -is, -e, cruel

cruentus, -a, -um, covered with blood, bloody

culmen, -inis (*n*), summit, height, top, roof-top

cum, when

cum (+ *abl.*), with

cumulus, -i (*m*), heap

cunctus, -a, -um, all

Cupido, -inis (*m*), Cupid (god of love)

cupressus, -i (*f*), cypress

cur? why?

cura, -ae (*f*), anxiety

curro, -ere, cucurri, cursum, to run

cursus, -us (*m*), running, journey, course

curvus, -a, -um, curved, winding

cuspis, -idis (*f*), spear

custos, -odis (*m*), guard

Cyclopeus, -a, -um, belonging to Cyclops (one-eyed giant)

Cyprus, -i (*f*), Cyprus (island in eastern Mediterranean)

Cythera, -orum (*n.pl*), Cythera (island in the Aegean)

Cythereus, -a, -um, of Cythera

D

Danai, -orum or **-um** (*m.pl*), the Danai, Greeks

daps, dapis (*f*), banquet

Dardania, -ae (*f*), Troy

Dardanidae, -um (*m.pl*), Trojans

Dardanius, -a, -um, Trojan

de (+ *abl.*), from, down from, about

dea, -ae (*f*), goddess

debeo (2), to owe

decem, ten

decorus, -a, -um, graceful

decurro, -ere, -curri, -cursum, to run down

decus, decoris (*n*), ornament

deduco, -ere, -duxi, -ductum, to lead, conduct (official word for leading to a new colony)

defendo, -ere, -di, -nsum, to defend

defensor, -oris (*m*), defender

defessus, -a, -um, weary, tired

deficio, -ere, -feci, -fectum, to fail, be wanting

defixus, -a, -um, immovable

degener, -eris, unworthy, disgraceful

dehinc, then

deinde, then

delabor, -i, -lapsus sum, to slip down, fall

delubrum, -i (*n*), shrine

demitto, -ere, -misi, -missum, to cast down, send down

demo, -ere, dempsi, demptum, to take away

demum, at long last

denique, at last, in short

densus, -a, -um, thick

depascor, -i, depastus sum, to feed on

descendo, -ere, -di, -nsum, to go down

desero, -ere, -ui, -rtum, to desert

desuetus, -a, -um, unaccustomed

desum, -esse, -fui, to be missing

desuper, from above

detineo, -ere, -ui, -tentum, to detain, hold back

deus, -i (*m*) (*nom.pl* **di**; *gen.pl* **deorum** or **deum**), god

devolvo, -ere, -volvi, -volutum, to roll down

devoveo, -ere, -vovi, -votum, to dedicate

dextra, -ae (*f*), right hand

Diana, -ae (f), Diana (goddess of hunting)
dicio, -onis (f), authority, rule
dictum, -i (n), word
Dido, -onis (f), Dido (queen of Carthage)
dies, -ei (m/f), day, daylight
diffugio, -ere, -fugi, to flee in different directions
dignus, -a, -um (+ abl.), worthy (of), deserved
digredior, -i, -gressus sum, to depart
dilectus, -a, -um, dear, loved, beloved
dimitto, -ere, -misi, -missum, to dismiss, send in different directions
Diomedes, -is (m), Diomede (Greek hero)
diripio, -ere, -ripui, -reptum, to plunder, tear in pieces
dirus, -a, -um, terrible, crazy
disco, -ere, didici (+ infin.), to learn (how to)
discrimen, -inis (n), critical moment, distinction
discumbo, -ere, -cubui, -cubitum, to recline
disicio, -ere, -ieci, -iectum, to scatter
dispello, -ere, -puli, -pulsum, to scatter
dissimulo (1), to hide, pretend, conceal (the fact of)
distendo, -ere, -di, -ntum, to stretch, swell out
diu, for a long time
diva, -ae (f), goddess
divello, -ere, -velli, -vulsum, to tear apart
diversus, -a, -um, in different directions
dives, divitis (+ gen.), rich (in)
divido, -ere, -visi, -visum, to divide, share
divinus, -a, -um, divine
divus, -i (m) (gen. pl divom), god
do, dare, dedi, datum, to give, grant, offer
vela dare, to set sail
doceo, -ere, -ui, doctum, to teach
Dolopes, -um (m.pl), the Dolopes, Greeks
dolor, -oris (m), sorrow, grief
dolus, -i (m), trick, trickery
dominor (1), to hold sway
domo, -are, domui, domitum, to subdue
domus, -us (f), house, home
donec, until
donum, -i (n), gift
Doricus, -a, -um, Doric, Greek
dorsum, -i (n), back, ridge, reef

draco, -onis (m), serpent
dubius, -a, -um, doubtful
duco, -ere, duxi, ductum, to lead, draw, bring, prolong
ductor, -onis (m), leader
dudum, before, lately
dulcis, -is, -e, sweet
dum, while
duo, duae, duo, two
duplex, -icis, double
duro (1), to be patient, persevere
durus, -a, -um, hard
dux, ducis (m), leader
Dymas, Dymantis (m), Dymas (father of Hecuba)

E

e, ex (+ abl.), out of, from
ex quo, from the moment when
ecce! behold!
edax, -acis, devouring
edissero, -ere, -ui, -rtum, to explain
educo, -ere, -duxi, -ductum, to lead out, raise up
effero, -ferre, extuli, elatum, to raise, bring out
effigies, -ei (f), image, statue
effodio, -ere, -fodi, -fossum, to excavate
effor, -fari, -fatus sum, to speak out, utter
effugio, -ere, -fugi, to escape
effundo, -ere, -fudi, -fusum, to pour out
egeo, -ere, -ui (+ abl.), to be in need (of), need
ego, I
mecum, with me
egredior, -i, -gressus sum, to disembark, go out
eicio, -ere, eieci, eiectum, to cast out
elabor, -i, elapsus sum, to slip out, escape
emitto, -ere, -misi, -missum, to let loose
emoveo, -ere, -movi, -motum, to move out, wrench from
enim, for
ensis, -is (m), sword
eo, ire, ivi or ii, itum, to go
Epeos, -i (m), Epeos (maker of the wooden horse)
epulae, -arum (f.pl), banquet, feast
Epytus, -i (m), Epytus (distinguished Trojan)
equidem, I for my part
equus, -i (m), horse
ergo, therefore
eripio, -ere, -ui, -reptum, to seize, snatch

erro (1), to wander
error, -oris (m), wandering, mistake,
  deception
erubesco, -ere, erubui, to begin to grow
  red, feel shame about
erumpo, -ere, -rupi, -ruptum, to burst,
  burst out
et, and, even, also
  et . . . et . . ., both . . . and . . .
etiam, also, even
Eurus, -i (m), the East Wind
evado, -ere, -vasi, -vasum, to escape,
  climb up
evenio, -ire, -veni, -ventum, to happen
everto, -ere, -verti, -versum, to
  overthrow
evinco, -ere, -vici, -victum, to conquer,
  overpower
ex (+ abl.), from, out of
exaudio (4), to hear
excedo, -ere, -cessi, -cessum, to depart
excidium, -i (n), destruction
excĭdo, -ere, -cĭdi, to fall from, cease
excīdo, -ere, -cīdi, -cīsum, to cut out,
  destroy
excito (1), to startle
exclamo (1), to shout out
excudo, -ere, -di, -sum, to strike out
excutio, -ere, -cussi, -cussum, to shake
  out, shake free
exeo, -ire, -ii, -itum, to go out
exerceo (2), to keep busy
exercitus, -us (m), army
exhalo (1), to breathe out
eximo, -ere, -emi, -emptum, to remove
exitialis, -is, -e, deadly, bringing
  destruction
exitium, -i (n), destruction
exorior, -iri, -ortus sum, to rise up
expedio (4), to prepare, get ready
  expedior (4), to make one's way
expello, -ere, -puli, -pulsum, to expel
expendo, -ere, -di, -nsum, to pay
  (penalty)
experior, -iri, -pertus sum, to try,
  experience
expleo, -ere, -evi, -etum, to satisfy
explico (1), to unfold
exploro (1), to try to discover
expromo, -ere, -prompsi, -promptum,
  to bring forth, utter
exsanguis, -is, -e, bloodless, pale, white
  (with fright)
exscindo, -ere, -scidi, -scissum, to
  destroy
exsilium, -i (n), exile

exspecto (1), to wait for
exsulto (1), to run riot, revel, boast
exsupero (1), to conquer, rise above
extemplo, immediately
extra (+ acc.), outside
extremus, -a, -um, last, farthest
extuli, see effero
exuo, -ere, -ui, -utum, to take off
exuviae, -arum (f.pl), spoils, armour

F

fabricator, -oris (m), builder
fabrico (1), to make, build
facies, -ei (f), appearance, shape
facilis, -is, -e, easy
facio, -ere, feci, factum, to make,
  force
factum, -i (n), deed
fallo, -ere, fefelli, falsum, to fail, let
  down, deceive
fama, -ae (f), story, fame, renown
fames, -is (f), hunger
famulus, -i (m), servant
fas est, it is right, it is allowed
fastigium, -i (n), roof-top
fatalis, -is, -e, fateful
fatisco, -ere, to gape
fatum, -i (n), fate
fatus, see for
fauces, -ium (f.pl), throat
fax, facis (f), torch
femineus, -a, -um, belonging to a
  woman
ferina, -ae (f), venison
ferio, -ire, to strike
fero, ferre, tuli, latum, to carry, bear,
  endure
  fertur, he makes his way
  ferunt, they say
  rapere et ferre, to loot and plunder
ferrum, -i (n), iron, sword
ferveo, -ere, ferbui, to boil, be in
  ferment
fessus, -a, -um, weary, tired
festino (1), to hurry, hasten
festus, -a, -um, festive, joyful
fetus, -a, -um, filled, full (of)
fetus, -us (m), offspring, young
fictus, -a, -um, false, feigned
fides, -ei (f), faith, honour, protection
fido, -ere, fisus sum (+ dat.), to trust
fiducia, -ae (f), confidence
fidus, -a, -um, faithful, trustworthy,
  sure (hope)
  male fida, treacherous
figo, -ere, fixi, fixum, to fix

filius, -i (*m*), son
finis, -is (*m*), end
  fines, -ium (*m.pl*), land, territory
fio, fieri, factus sum, to be made, take
  place, happen
firmo (1), to confirm
fixus, -a, -um, determined
flagro (1), to burn, blaze
flamma, -ae (*f*), flame
flecto, -ere, flexi, flexum, to bend, turn
fleo, -ere, flevi, fletum, to weep
fletus, -us (*m*), weeping, tears
floreus, -a, -um, flowery
flos, floris (*m*), flower
fluctus, -us (*m*), wave, sea
flumen, -inis (*n*), river, stream
fluo, -ere, fluxi, fluxum, to flow, ebb
fluvius, -i (*m*), river
foedo (1), to make foul, disfigure,
  outrage
folium, -i (*n*), leaf
fomes, -itis (*m*), kindling-wood, tinder
fons, fontis (*m*), fountain, (in *plural*)
  water
for, fari, fatus sum, to speak, say
foris, -is (*f*), door
forma, -ae (*f*), beauty
formido, -inis (*f*), fear
forsan, perhaps
forsitan, perhaps
forte, as it so happened
  si forte in the hope that
fortis, -is, -e, brave
fortuna, -ae (*f*), chance, fortune
fortunatus, -a, -um, fortunate
foveo, -ere, fovi, fotum, to cherish
fragor, -oris (*m*), crash
fragrans, -antis, sweet-smelling
frango, -ere, fregi, fractum, to break,
  grind
frater, fratris (*m*), brother
fremitus, -us (*m*), roaring
fremo, -ere, -ui, -itum, to roar
freno (1), to restrain
frequentes, -es, -ia, in crowds
fretum, -i (*n*), strait, sea
frondeus, -a, -um, leafy
frons, frondis (*f*), foliage, leafy branch
fruges, -um (*f.pl*), grain
frustra, in vain
frustum, -i (*n*), slice
fuga, -ae (*f*), flight
fugio, -ere, fugi, fugitum, to flee
fugo (1), to put to flight
fulgeo, -ere, fulsi, to gleam, shine
fulvus, -a, -um, yellow, tawny

fundamentum, -i (*n*), foundation
fundo, -ere, fudi, fusum, to spread,
  scatter, pour
funis, -is (*m*), rope
funus, -eris (*n*), funeral, death
furiatus, -a, -um, frenzied
furo, -ere, -ui, to rage
furor, -oris (*m*), frenzy, madness
furtim, stealthily
futurus, -a, -um, coming, future

G

galea, -ae (*f*), helmet
gaudeo, -ere, gavisus sum, to rejoice
gaza, -ae (*f*), treasure
gemini, -ae, -a, twin, two
gemitus, -us (*m*), groan
gemma, -ae (*f*), jewel
gemo, -ere, -ui, -itum, to groan, groan
  over, bemoan, lament
gener, -i (*m*), son-in-law
genetrix, -icis (*f*), mother
genitor, -oris (*m*), father
gens, gentis (*f*), race
genus, generis (*n*), race, kind
gero, -ere, gessi, gestum, to carry, bear,
  wear
gigno, -ere, genui, genitum, to bear (a
  child)
glaeba, -ae (*f*), soil
glomero (1), to assemble, crowd round
gloria, -ae (*f*), glory
gradior, -i, gressus sum, to walk
gradus, -us (*m*), step
Grai, -orum (*m.pl*), Greeks
Graius, -a, -um, Greek
grates (*f.pl*), thanks
gratus, -a, -um, welcome
gravis, -is, -e, serious
graviter, heavily
gravo (1), to burden
gremium, -i (*n*), lap, bosom
gressus, -us (*m*), step
gurges, -itis (*m*), whirlpool, flood
Gyas, -ae (*m*), Gyas (companion of
  Aeneas)

H

habeo (2), to have, hold
haereo, -ere, haesi, haesum, to stick,
  cling, remain fixed
harena, -ae (*f*), *sand*
hasta, -ae (*f*), spear
hastile, -is (*n*), spear
haud, not
Hector, -oris (*m*), Hector (son of Priam)

Hectoreus, -a, -um, of Hector, belonging to Hector
Hecuba, -ae (*f*), Hecuba (wife of Priam)
hei! alas!
 hei mihi! ah me!
Helena, -ae (*f*), Helen (wife of Menelaus who was carried off by Paris)
herba, -ae (*f*), grass
Hesperia, -ae (*f*), Hesperia (the land in the west)
heu! alas!
hic, here, hereupon
hic, haec, hoc, this
hiems, hiemis (*f*), winter, storm
hinc, from here, after this
 hinc atque hinc, on this side and on that, all round
hodie, today
homo, -inis (*m*), man
honos, honoris (*m*), honour, grace, charm, thank-offering
horrendus, -a, -um, dreadful
horreo (2), to bristle, shudder
horresco, -ere, horrui, to begin to shudder
horror, -oris (*m*), horror
hortor (1), to urge
hospes, -itis (*m*), guest
hostis, -is (*m*), enemy
huc, here, to this place
humi, on the ground
hymenaeus, -i (*m*), marriage
Hypanis, -is (*m*), Hypanis (a Trojan)

I

iactatus, -a, -um, tossed about
iacto (1), to fling, toss
 se iactare, to boast
iactura, -ae (*f*), loss
iam, now, already
 iam pridem, now for a long time
iamdudum, a long time
ianua, -ae (*f*), door
ibi, there, at that point
ictus, -us (*m*), blow
Ida, -ae (*f*), Mount Ida (near Troy)
Idalia, -ae (*f*),
Idalium, -i (*n*)
 } a mountain city in Cyprus where Venus had a temple
idem, eadem, idem, the same
ignarus, -a, -um, ignorant
ignis, -is (*m*), fire
Iliacus, -a, -um, Trojan
ilicet, immediately

Ilione, -es (*f*), Ilione (daughter of Priam)
Ilioneus, -i (*m*), Ilioneus (follower of Aeneas)
Ilium, -i (*n*), Troy
ille, illa, illud, he, she, it; that
illic, there
imago, -inis (*f*), image, form, picture, vision
imbellis, -is, -e, unwarlike
imber, imbris (*m*), rain, water
immanis, -is, -e, huge, wild, fierce
immemor, -oris, unmindful
immensus, -a, -um, huge
immineo, -ere, to loom over
immitis, -is, -e, merciless
immo, nay rather
impello, -ere, -puli, -pulsum, to strike, drive on, push over
imperium, -i (*n*), power
impius, -a, -um, wicked, impious
impleo, -ere, -evi, -etum, to fill, satisfy
implico, -are, -ui, -itum, to entwine, enfold
impono, -ere, -posui, -positum, to place upon
improvidus, -a, -um, not foreseeing
improvisus, -a, -um, unexpected, unforeseen
imus, -a, -um, lowest, bottom of
 ex imo, from its foundations
in (+ *abl.*), in, on
in (+ *acc.*) into, against
incedo, -ere, -cessi, -cessum, to walk
incendium, -i (*n*), fire
incendo, -ere, -di, -nsum, to set on fire
inceptum, -i (*n*), understanding, purpose, resolve
incertus, -a, -um, uncertain, ill-aimed
incido, -ere, -cidi, -casum, to fall on
incipio, -ere, -cepi, -ceptum, to begin
includo, -ere, -clusi, -clusum, to shut in
inclutus, -a, -um, famous
incognitus, -a, -um, unknown
inconcessus, -a, -um, not allowed, unlawful
incubo, -are, -cubui, -cubitum, to settle on
incumbo, -ere, -cubui, -cubitum, to settle upon; (+ *dat.*) to add weight (to)
incurro, -ere, -curri, -cursum, to run in
incutio, -ere, -cussi, -cussum, to strike
inde, from there, then
indico, -ere, -dixi, -dictum, to proclaim
indignor (1), to be angry

indignus, -a, -um, unworthy, cruel
indulgeo, -ere, -dulsi, -dultum (+ *dat.*), to give way (to)
induo, -ere, -ui, -utum, to put on
indutus, -a, -um, clad, having donned, having put on
ineluctabilis, -is, -e, inevitable, inescapable
inermis, -is, -e, unarmed
iners, inertis, lifeless, motionless
infandus, -a, -um, unspeakable, dreadful
infelix, -icis, unlucky, luckless, unhappy
infensus, -a, -um, hostile
infestus, -a, -um, hostile, dangerous
infula, -ae (*f*), headband
ingemino (1), to redouble
ingens, -ntis, huge, mighty, great
inicio, -ere, -ieci, -iectum, to fling into
inimicus, -a, -um, hostile
iniuria, -ae (*f*), insult
inlabor, -i, -lapsus sum, to glide in
inludo, -eré, -lusi, -lusum, to mock
inmitto, -ere, -misi, -missum, to send in
inmixtus, -a, -um, intermingled
innoxius, -a, -um, harmless
innuptus, -a, -um, unmarried
inquit, he (she) says, said
inrigo (1), to irrigate, diffuse
inruo, -ere, -ui, to rush in
insania, -ae (*f*), madness
insanus, -a, -um, mad
inscius, -a, -um, not knowing, unaware
insequor, -i, -secutus sum, to follow, pursue
inserto (1), to put into, insert
insidiae, -arum (*f. pl*), ambush, trap, guiles, tricks
insido, -ere, -sedi, -sessum, to settle in, take possession
insigne, -is (*n*), distinctive mark, badge
insinuo (1), to wind one's way into, creep into
insono, -are, -ui, to resound, sound loudly
inspiro (1), to breathe into, excite
instar (*indeclinable neuter*), a likeness
instauro (1), to renew
insterno, -ere, -stravi, -stratum, to cover over
insto, -are, -stiti, -statum, to press on
instruo, -ere, -struxi, -structum, to draw up, decorate
insula, -ae (*f*), island

intendo, -ere, -di, -nsum, to draw tight, stretch
intentus, -a, -um, attentive
inter (+ *acc.*), between, among
interdum, sometimes, at times
interea, meanwhile
interior, -ius, inner, the inside of
intono, -are, -ui, to thunder
intorqueo, -ere, -rsi, -rtum, to hurl against
intra (+ *acc.*), inside
introgredior, -i, -gressus sum, to enter
intus, within, inside
inultus, -a, -um, unavenged
inutilis, -is, -e, useless
invado, -ere, -vasi, -vasum, to go against, attack
invenio, -ire, -veni, -ventum, to find
inventor, -oris (*m*), deviser, contriver
invisus, -a, -um, hated
invitus, -a, -um, unwilling
involvo, -ere, -volvi, -volutum, to wrap, enfold
ipse, ipsa, ipsum, -self
ira, -ae (*f*), anger
irritus, -a, -um, useless, to no purpose
is, ea, id, he, she, it; that
iste, ista, istud, that
ita, thus, in this way
Italia, -ae (*f*), Italy
iter, itineris (*n*), way, road
iterum, again
iuba, -ae (*f*), crest, plume
iubeo, -ere, iussi, iussum, to order
iudicium, -i (*n*), judgement
iugum, -i (*n*), ridge
Iulus, -i (*m*), Iulus (son of Aeneas; also called Ascanius)
iungo, -ere, iunxi, iunctum, to join, unite
Iuno, -onis (*f*), Juno (queen of the gods and wife of Jupiter)
Iuppiter, Iovis (*m*), Jupiter (king of the gods; sometimes called Jove)
ius, iuris (*n*), right, law, justice
iussu (+ *gen.*), by order (of)
iussum, -i (*n*), order, command
iustitia, -ae (*f*), justice
iustus, -a, -um, just, fair
iuvat, it gives pleasure
iuvenilis, -is, -e, youthful
iuvenis, -is (*m*), (young) man
iuventa, -ae (*f*), youth
iuventus, -utis (*f*), youth
iuvo, -are, iuvi, iutum, to help
iuxta, nearby

L

labo (1), to totter
labor, -i, lapsus sum, to slip, glide
labor, -oris (*m*), work, labour, task, toil, hardship, trouble
laboro (1), to work
lacrima, -ae (*f*), tear
lacrimo (1), to weep
laedo, -ere, laesi, laesum, to harm, insult
laetitia, -ae (*f*), joy
laetus, -a, -um, joyful, glad, festive
laeva, -ae (*f*), left hand
laevus, -a, -um, on the left
lambo, -ere, -bi, to lick
Laocoon, -ontis (*m*), Laocoon (son of Priam and Priest of Apollo)
lapso (1), to slip
lapsus, -us (*m*), gliding, slipping
largus, -a, -um, plentiful
Larissaeus, -a, -um, belonging to Larissa (town in Thessaly)
lassus, -a, -um, weary
late, widely, far and wide
latebrae, -arum (*f.pl*), hiding place
lateo (2), to lie in hiding
latex, -icis (*m*), liquid, fluid
Latium, -i (*n*), Latium (the part of Italy where Rome lies)
latus, -a, -um, broad, wide
latus, -eris (*n*), side
laurus, -i (*f*), laurel tree
laus, laudis (*f*), praise, glory
Lavinus, -a, -um, belonging to Lavinium
laxo (1), to loosen
laxus, -a, -um, loose
Leda, -ae (*f*), Leda (mother of Helen)
lego, -ere, legi, lectum, to choose
lenis, -is, -e, gentle
leo, leonis (*m*), lion
letum, -i (*n*), death
levis, -is, -e, light, flickering
levo (1), to loosen, lighten, relieve
lex, legis (*f*), law
Libya, -ae (*f*), Libya, Africa
Libycus, -a, -um, Libyan
lignum, -i (*n*), wood, anything made of wood
ligo (1), to bind
limen, -inis (*n*), door, doorway, threshold
lingua, -ae (*f*), tongue
liqueo, -ere, liqui, to be liquid
litus, litoris (*n*), shore
loco (1), to place

locus, -i (*m*) (*pl.* **loca**), place
longaevus, -a, -um, aged
longe, far off, at a distance
longus, -a, -um, long
loquor, -i, locutus sum, to speak
Lucifer, -eri (*m*), Lucifer (the morning star)
luctor (1), to struggle
luctus, -us (*m*), grief
lucus, -i (*m*), grove, wood
lumen, -inis (*n*), light
lumina, -um (*n. pl*), eyes
luna, -ae (*f*), moon
lustro (1), to search, survey, traverse, make one's way through
lux, lucis (*f*), light
luxus, -us (*m*), luxury
Lyaeus, -i (*m*), the Relaxer (a name given to Bacchus)
Lydius, -a, -um, Lydian
lympha, -ae (*f*), water

M

Machaon, -onis (*m*), Machaon (famous surgeon)
machina, -ae (*f*), machine, engine
macto (1), to sacrifice
maereo (2), to be sad, mourn
maestus, -a, -um, sad, dejected, gloomy
magalia, -ium (*n.pl*), huts
magis, more
magnus, -a, -um, great, big (**maior, maximus,** greater, greatest)
male, badly
   male amicus, hostile
   male fida, treacherous
malum, -i (*n*), misfortune
maneo, -ere, mansi, mansum, to remain, await
mantele, -is (*n*), towel
manicae, -arum (*f.pl*), handcuffs
manus, -us (*f*), hand, band
mare, maris (*n*), sea
mater, matris (*f*), mother
maturo (1), to hasten
maximus, -a, -um, biggest, mightiest, oldest
medius, -a, -um, middle, the middle
mel, mellis (*n*), honey
melior, -ius, better
membrum, -i (*n*), limb
memini, -isse, to remember
   memento! remember!
memor, -oris, mindful
memoro (1), to speak
Menelaus, -i (*m*), Menelaus (brother of Agamemnon and husband of Helen)

mens, mentis (*f*), mind, thought, support
mensa, -ae (*f*), table
mentior (4), to lie, tell lies
mereor (2), to deserve
metus, -us (*m*), fear
meus, -a, -um, my
mico, -are, -ui, to gleam
miles, -itis (*m*), soldier, company of
soldiers
mille, a thousand
Minerva, -ae (*f*), Minerva (goddess of
wisdom and war)
ministro (1), to tend to
minor (1), to threaten, menace
minus, less
  nec minus, also
mirabilis, -is, -e, wonderful
  mirabile dictu, wonderful to relate
miror (1), to marvel at
misceo, -ere, -ui, mixtum, to mix,
trouble
miser, -era, -erum, wretched
miserabilis, -is, -e, wretched, pitiable
  miserabile visu, a pitiful sight to see
misereor (2), to pity
miseresco, -ere, to feel pity for
miseror (1), to pity
mitto, -ere, misi, missum, to send, put
away, put an end to
moenia, -ium (*n. pl*), walls, walled city,
city buildings
moles, -is (*f*), massive bulk, task, bank
(of river)
molior (4), to build, work upon
mollio (4), to soften, soothe
mollis, -is, -e, soft
moneo (2), to advise
monile, -is (*n*), necklace
mons, montis (*m*), mountain
monstro (1), to show
monstrum, -i (*n*), omen, miracle,
monster
montanus, -a, -um, of a mountain
mora, -ae (*f*), delay
morior, mori, mortuus sum, to die
  moriturus, -a, -um, about to die,
determined to die
moror (1), to delay
mors, mortis (*f*), death
morsus, -us (*m*), bite
mortalis, -is, -e, mortal
moveo, -ere, movi, motum, to move
mucro, -onis (*m*), sword
mugitus, -us (*m*), bellowing, lowing
mulceo, -ere, mulsi, mulsum, to soothe,
comfort

multum, much
multus, -a, -um, much
  multi, -ae, -a, many
munus, -eris (*n*), gift
murmur, -uris (*n*), rumbling
murus, -i (*m*), wall
muto (1), to change
Mycenae, -arum (*f.pl*), Mycenae
(Agamemnon's city)
Mygdonides, -ae (*m*), Mygdonides (the
son of Mygdon)
Myrmidones, -um (*m.pl*), the
Myrmidons (people in Thessaly ruled
by Achilles)

N

nam, for
namque, for
narro (1), to tell
nata, -ae (*f*), daughter
natus, -i (*m*), son
  nate dea, o you who are born of a
goddess
navis, -is (*f*), ship
ne (+ *subj.*), lest, in case
ne credite! do not trust!
nec, and . . . not, nor
  nec . . . nec . . ., neither . . . nor
  . . .
  nec minus, also
  nec non et, also
necdum, and not yet
nectar, -aris (*n*), nectar (the drink of
the gods)
nefas, sacrilege
nemus, -oris (*n*), grove
Neoptolemus, -i (*m*), Neoptolemus (son
of Achilles; also called Pyrrhus)
nepos, -otis (*m*), grandson
Neptunius, -a, -um, built by Neptune
Neptunus, -i (*m*), Neptune (god of the
sea)
neque, and . . . not, nor
  neque . . . neque . . ., neither . . .
  nor . . .
  neque enim, for indeed . . . not
nequeo, -ire, -ivi, -itum, to be unable
nequiquam, in vain, idly
nescio (4), not to know
  nescio quod, some . . . or other
ni, unless
nihil, nothing
nimbosus, -a, -um, rainy, stormy
nimbus, -i (*m*), rain-storm, thunder-
cloud
nitor, -i, nixus sum, to strive

no (1), to swim
nodus, -i (*m*), knot
nomen, -inis (*n*), name, reputation
non, not
   nec non et, also
nos, we, us
noster, -tra, -trum, our
   nostri, -orum (*m.pl*), our men
notus, -a, -um, known, well-known
Notus, -i (*m*), South Wind, any wind
novus, -a, -um, new
nox, noctis (*f*), night
nubes, -is (*f*), cloud
nudo (1), to lay bare
nudus, -a, -um, naked, open
nullus, -a, -um, no, none
numen, -inis (*n*), divine power, divine
   purpose, deity
numerus, -i (*m*), number
numquam, never
nunc, now
nuntius, -i (*m*), messenger, message
nurus, -us (*f*), daughter-in-law
nutrimentum, -i (*n*), nourishment, fuel

O

ob (+ *acc.*), on account of
obicio, -ere, -ieci, -iectum, to fling to,
   present against
oblatus, *see* **offero**
obliviscor, -i, oblitus sum, to forget
obruo, -ere, -ui, -utum, to overwhelm
obscurus, -a, -um, dark
observo (1), to watch, observe
obsideo, -ere, -sedi, -sessum, to besiege,
   block
obstipesco, -ere, -pui, to be amazed
obtutus, -us (*m*), fixed gaze
occulto (1), to hide
occultus, -a, -um, hidden, secret
occurro, -ere, -curri, -cursum (+ *dat.*),
   to meet, come to meet
oceanus, -i (*m*), sea, ocean
oculus, -i (*m*), eye
offero, offerre, obtuli, oblatum, to offer
   se offert, he comes to meet
olim, once, one day
Olympus, -i (*m*), Mount Olympus
omen, ominis (*n*), omen, sign
omnipotens, -entis, all-powerful,
   almighty
omnis, -is, -e, all, whole, every
onero (1), to load
onus, oneris (*n*), load, burden
opacus, -a, -um, shady
opimus, -a, -um, rich

ops, opis (*f*), help
   opes, opum (*f.pl*), wealth, resources
oppono, -ere, -posui, -positum, to place
   in the way
oppositus, -a, -um, resisting
opprimo, -ere, -pressi, -pressum, to
   overwhelm
opto (1), to wish, desire, choose
opus, operis (*n*), work, task
ora, -ae (*f*), shore
orbis, -is (*m*), coil, circle, rim
Orcus, -i (*m*), the Underworld
ordior, -iri, orsus sum, to begin
ordo, -inis (*m*), row, rank, line
oreas, -adis (*f*), mountain nymph
origo, -inis (*f*), origin, beginning
Orion, -onis (*m*), Orion (a constellation
   whose rising and setting frequently
   bring storms)
orior, -iri, ortus sum, to arise
ornatus, -us (*m*), splendid attire
oro (1), to beg
os, oris (*n*), face, mouth, eyes
os, ossis (*n*), bone
osculum, -i (*n*), kiss
ostendo, -ere, -di, -nsum, to show
ostrum, -i (*n*), purple
Othryades, -ae (*m*), Panthus (the son of
   Othrys)

P

palla, -ae (*f*), cloak
Palladium, -i (*n*), statue of Pallas
   Athene
Pallas, -adis (*f*), Pallas Athene (Greek
   name for Minerva, the goddess of
   wisdom and war)
palma, -ae (*f*), palm (of hand)
pando, -ere, pandi, passum, to open,
   unfold
Panthus, -i (*m*), Panthus (nephew of
   Hecuba)
par, paris (+ *dat.*), like, equal (to)
paratus, -a, -um, prepared, ready
parco, -ere, peperci, parsum (+ *dat.*),
   to spare
parens, -ntis (*m/f*), parent
pareo (2) (+ *dat.*), to obey
paries, -etis (*m*), wall
pario, -ere, peperi, partum, to produce,
   gain
Paris, -idis (*m*), Paris (son of Priam)
pariter, equally, side by side
paro (1), to prepare
pars, partis (*f*), part, some . . . others
   . . .

partior (4), to share, distribute
parvus, -a, -um, small, tiny
pasco, -ere, pavi, pastum, to feed
passim, everywhere
passis crinibus, with dishevelled hair
passus, -us (*m*), step
pastor, -oris (*m*), shepherd
patefacio, -ere, -feci, -factum, to (make) open
pateo (2), to be open
pater, patris (*m*), father, lord
  patres, -um (*m.pl*), ancestors
patesco, -ere, patui, to begin to be open
patior, pati, passus sum, to suffer, endure
patria, -ae (*f*), native land
patrius, -a, -um, belonging to a father or fatherland, a father's
pauci, -ae, -a, few
paulatim, little by little, gradually
pavidus, -a, -um, terrified
pavito (1), to be in great fear
pavor, -oris (*m*), fear, panic
pectus, -oris (*n*), breast, heart, mind
pelagus, -i (*n*), sea
Pelasgus, -a, -um, Pelasgian, Greek
Pelides, -ae (*m*), Achilles (son of Peleus)
pellis, -is (*f*), skin, hide
pello, -ere, pepuli, pulsum, to drive away
Pelopeus, -a, -um, belonging to Pelops, Greek
Penates, -ium (*m.pl*), Household Gods
pendeo, -ere, pependi, to hang
penetralia, -ium (*n.pl*), chambers, interior (of building)
penitus, deep(ly), from the innermost depths
per (+ *acc.*), through, over, across
percussus, -a, -um, struck
pereo, -ire, -ii, -itum, to perish, die
perflo (1), to blow through or over
Pergama, -orum (*n.pl*), the citadel of Troy, Troy
periculum, -i (*n*), (contracted to **periclum** in LDOT 424), danger
Periphas, -antis (*m*), Periphas (one of the companions of Pyrrhus)
periurus, -a, -um, false, lying
perrumpo, -ere, -rupi, -ruptum, to break through
persolvo, -ere, -solvi, -solutum, to pay to the full
persono, -are, -ui, -itum, to sound

persto, -are, -stiti, -statum, to persist, stand firm
pervenio, -ire, -veni, -ventum, to arrive
pes, pedis (*m*), foot
pestis, -is (*f*), ruin, destruction
peto, -ere, -ivi, -itum, to seek, look for, want, make for, head for
phalanx, -angis (*f*), phalanx, dense mass of troops
pharetra, -ae (*f*), quiver (for arrows)
Phoebus, -i (*m*), Phoebus Apollo (god of divination and light)
Phoenissus, -a, -um, Phoenician
Phoenix, -icis (*m*), Phoenix (companion of Achilles)
Phryges, -um (*m.pl*), Phrygians
Phrygius, -a, -um, Phrygian
pictus, -a, -um, embroidered
pietas, -atis (*f*), goodness
pineus, -a, -um, made of pine
pinguis, -is, -e, fat, rich
pio (1), to atone for
pius, -a, -um, noble-hearted
placeo (2) (+ *dat.*), to please
  placet (+ *dat.*), it is the will (of)
placidus, -a, -um, calm, serene
placo (1), to calm
plangor, -oris (*m*), mourning, beating of breast
plausus, -us (*m*), applause
plurimus, -a, -um, very much, very big
  plurimi, -ae, -a, very many
poena, -ae (*f*), punishment
poenas dare, to pay the penalty
Polites, -ae (*m*), Polites (son of Priam)
polus, -i (*m*), sky, heaven
pone, behind
pono, -ere, posui, positum, to place
pontus, -i (*m*), sea
populo (1), to devastate, ravage
populor (1), to devastate, ravage
porta, -ae (*f*), gate, opening
porticus, -us (*m*), colonnade, cloister
porto (1), to carry
portus, -us (*m*), harbour
posco, -ere, poposci, to demand, ask for
possum, posse, potui, to be able, (can)
post (+ *acc.*), after, behind
post (*adv.*), afterwards, then
postis, -is (*m*), doorpost, door
postquam, after
potens, -ntis, powerful
potentia, -ae (*f*), might, power
potior (4) (+ *abl.*), to take possession (of)

praeceps, -cipitis, headlong
in praecipiti, on the sheer edge, above a sheer drop
praecipito (1), to hurl, urge on
praecipue, especially
praecordia, -orum (n.pl), heart
praeda, -ae (f), booty, spoil, prey
praemitto, -ere, -misi, -missum, to send on, send ahead
praemium, -i, (n), reward
praeruptus, -a, -um, steep, sheer
praeterea, besides
praeverto, -ere, -ti, -rsum, to anticipate, take possession of beforehand
preces, -um (f.pl), prayers
premo, -ere, pressi, pressum, to press, hold in check, strike
prendo, -ere, -di, -nsum, to hold
prenso (1), to grasp firmly
Priameius, -a, -um, belonging to Priam
Priamus, -i (m), Priam (king of Troy)
pridem, see iam pridem
primo, at first
primum, first, firstly
ut primum, as soon as
primus, -a, -um, first
principio, in the beginning, first of all
prior, prius, first
prius (adv.), first
priusquam, until
pro (+ abl.), in return for, in place of, to atone for
procedo, -ere, -cessi, -cessum, to go forward
procella, -ae (f), storm
procul, at a distance
procumbo, -ere, -cubui, -cubitum, to fall forward, fall flat
produco, -ere, -duxi, -ductum, to prolong
proelium, -i (n), battle
profor, -fari, -fatus sum, to speak out
profugus, -a, -um, fleeing
profundus, -a, -um, deep
progenies, -ei (f), offspring
prohibeo (2), to hold back, avert
promo, -ere, prompsi, promptum, to bring out
prope (+ acc.), near
propinquo (1) (+ dat.), to approach
prora, -ae (f), prow
prosequor, -i, -secutus sum, to accompany, continue speaking
prospectus, -us (m), view, scene
prospicio, -ere, -spexi, -spectum, to look forth, see

protego, -ere, -xi, -ctum, to protect
protinus, immediately, forthwith
proveho, -ere, -vexi, -vectum, to carry forward
provehor, -i, -vectus sum, to sail
proximus, -a, -um, nearest
pubes, -is (f), youth, crowd of youths
puella, -ae (f), girl.
puer, -i (m), boy (plural: children)
pugna, -ae (f), battle
pulcher, -chra, -chrum, beautiful
puppis, -is (f), stern, ship
purgo (1), to clear, free
purpureus, -a, -um, purple, bright, shining
puto (1), to think
Pyrrhus, -i (m), Pyrrhus (son of Achilles; also called Neoptolemus)

Q

qua, where
quaero, -ere, quaesivi, quaesitum, to seek, ask, question, investigate
qualis, -is, -e, what sort of, just like
quamquam, although
quantum, how much
quantus, -a, -um, how great, how powerful
quare, therefore
quater, four times
-que, and
-que . . . -que . . ., (both) . . . and . . .
qui, quae, quod (relative pronoun), who, which
qui? quae? quod? (interrogative adjective), which? what?
quicunque, quaecunque, quodcunque, whoever, whatever
quid? why?
quies, -etis (f), rest
quietus, -a, -um, peaceful
quin etiam, nay more
quinquaginta, fifty
quippe, certainly, in as much as
quis, quis, quid, any
si quis, if anyone
quis? quis? quid? who? what?
quisquam, quaequam, quicquam, anyone, anything
quisquis, quisquis, quicquid, whoever, whatever
quisque, quaeque, quodque, each
quo, where, whither
quocunque, wherever
quondam, once, formerly
quoque, also

R

rabies (*acc.* **rabiem**) (*f*), rage, fierceness
rapidus, -a, -um, swift
rapio, -ere, -ui, raptum, to seize, catch, take, carry off, plunder
rarus, -a, -um, scattered, here and there
ratio, -onis (*f*), reason
raucus, -a, -um, hoarse, hollow-sounding
recedo, -ere, -cessi, -cessum, to recede, draw back
recens, -entis, recent, fresh
recipio, -ere, -cepi, -ceptum, to receive, take back, take in, rescue
recondo, -ere, -didi, -ditum, to hide
rectus, -a, -um, straight, upright
recuso (1), to refuse
recutio, -ere, -cussi, -cussum, to strike back
reddo, -ere, -didi, -ditum, to give back
redeo, -ire, -ii, -itum, to go back, return
redoleo (2), to give off a scent, smell
reduco, -ere, -duxi, -ductum, to bring back
refero, -ferre, rettuli, relatum, to take back, utter (words)
  me refero, I return
reflecto, -ere, -flexi, -flexum, to bend back, cast back
refugio, -ere, -fugi, to shrink back
refulgeo, -ere, -fulsi, to shine brightly
regalis, -is, -e, royal
regina, -ae (*f*), queen
regio, -onis (*f*), direction
regius, -a, -um, royal
regnator, -oris (*m*), ruler
regno (1), to reign, rule
regnum, -i (*n*), kingdom, realm
religio, -onis (*f*), religious rite or observance
religiosus, -a, -um, holy
relinquo, -ere, -liqui, -lictum, to leave, abandon
reliquiae, -arum (*f.pl*), remnant
remitto, -ere, -misi, -missum, to send back
removeo, -ere, -movi, -motum, to remove
remus, -i (*m*), oar
renovo (1), to renew, revive
reor, reri, ratus sum, to think
repello, -ere, reppuli, repulsum, to drive back
repente, suddenly

repeto, -ere, -ivi, -itum, to seek again
repleo, -ere, -evi, -etum, to fill
repono, -ere, -posui, -positum, to store
reprimo, -ere, -pressi, -pressum, to keep back, check
requiro, -ere, -quisivi, -quisitum, to search for, seek to know, ask
res, rei (*f*), thing, story, event
  res laetae, prosperity
  res secundae, success, prosperous times
reses, residis, inactive
resido, -ere, -sedi, to sit down
resisto, -ere, -stiti (+ *dat.*), to resist, stand still
respecto (1), to look back, respect
respicio, -ere, -spexi, -spectum, to look back
respondeo, -ere, -di, -nsum (+ *dat.*), to reply (to), agree (with), conform (with/to)
responsum, -i (*n*), reply
restinguo, -ere, -nxi, -nctum, to put out (a fire)
resto, -are, -stiti, to remain, be left over
resurgo, -ere, -surrexi, -surrectum, to rise again
retro, backwards
revincio, -ire, -vinxi, -vinctum, to bind
reviso, -ere, -visi, -visum, to revisit
revoco (1), to recall
rex, regis (*m*), king
Rhipeus, -i (*m*), Rhipeus (a companion of Aeneas)
rigens, -entis, stiff
rima, -ae (*f*), crack
ripa, -ae (*f*), bank (of river)
robur, roboris (*n*), oak
rogito (1), to ask eagerly, ask repeatedly
rogo (1), to ask
Romanus, -a, -um, Roman
rota, -ae (*f*), wheel
rudens, -ntis (*m*), rope
ruina, -ae (*f*), ruin, downpour
rumpo, -ere, rupi, ruptum, to burst
ruo, -ere, rui, to rush, churn up
rupes, -is (*f*), rock
rursus, again
rus, ruris (*n*), country, countryside

S

sacer, -cra, -crum, sacred
  sacra, -orum (*n.pl*), sacred emblems, sacred rites

sacerdos, -otis (*m*), priest
sacratus, -a, -um, made holy, hallowed
sacro (1), to make holy
saeculum, -i (*n*), age, generation, race, breed
saeptus, -a, -um, surrounded
saevus, -a, -um, fierce, cruel
sagitta, -ae (*f*), arrow
sal, salis (*n*), salt, salt water, salt sea
salum, -i (*n*), sea
salus, -utis (*f*), safety
sanctus, -a, -um, holy
sanguis, -inis (*m*), blood
sat = satis, enough, sufficient
sata, -orum (*n.pl*), crops
Saturnius, -a, -um, belonging to Saturn
satus, -a, -um, born, sprung from
saucius, -a, -um, wounded
saxum, -i (*n*), rock, stone
scaena, -ae (*f*), stage
scala, -ae (*f*), ladder
scando, -ere, -di, -nsum, to climb
sceleratus, -a, -um, guilty, accursed
scelus, -eris (*n*), crime
sceptrum, -i (*n*), sceptre
scindo, -ere, -scidi, scissum, to tear asunder
scintilla, -ae (*f*), spark
scio (4), to know
scitor (1), to ask, enquire
scopulus, -i (*m*), rock
Scyllaeus, -a, -um, belonging to Scylla (dangerous rock in straits between Italy and Sicily)
se *or* **sese,** himself, herself, itself, themselves
secludo, -ere, -si, -sum, to shut off
seco, -are, -ui, sectum, to cut
secundus, -a, -um, favourable, prosperous
  res secundae, success, prosperous times
securis, -is (*f*), axe
secus, otherwise
sed, but
  sed enim, however
sedeo, -ere, sedi, sessum, to sit
sedes, -is (*f*), seat, position, place, home
seges, -etis (*f*), cornfield
segnities (*f*), slowness
semper, always
senior, -oris, aged; old man (= **senex**)
sententia, -ae (*f*), thought, opinion
sentio, -ire, sensi, sensum, to realise
sentis, -is (*m*), thorn

sepelio, -ire, -ivi, sepultum, to bury
septem, seven
septimus, -a, -um, seventh
sepulchrum, -i (*n*), tomb
sequor, -i, secutus sum, to follow
serenus, -a, -um, clear, fair, calm
Sergestus, -i (*m*), Sergestus (Trojan helmsman)
series (*no gen.*) (*f*), succession
sermo, -onis (*m*), speech, conversation
serpens, -ntis (*m*), serpent, snake
serpo, -ere, serpsi, serptum, to creep
serus, -a, -um, late
servio (4) (+ *dat.*), to be a slave (to)
servo (1), to keep, keep safe, protect, preserve
sese = se
seu, whether, or
si, if
  si forte, in the hope that
  si quis, if anyone
sibilus, -a, -um, hissing
sic, thus, in this way, as follows
Siculus, -a, -um, Sicilian
Sidonius, -a, -um, from Sidon (ancient Phoenician city)
sidus, sideris (*n*), star
signum, -i (*n*), sign, marking, figure
silentium, -i (*n*), silence
silex, silicis (*m*), flint
silva, -ae (*f*), wood
similis, -is, -e, similar, like
Simois, Simoentis (*m*), Simois (small river near Troy)
simul, at the same time, together
simulacrum, -i (*n*), image, statue
simulo (1), to pretend, feign
sin, but if
sine (+ *abl.*), without
sinistra, -ae (*f*), left hand
sino, -ere, sivi, situm, to allow
Sinon, -onis (*m*), Sinon (the Greek who told the tale of the Wooden Horse to the Trojans)
sinus, -us (*m*), bay
sisto, -ere, stiti, to place, set
sit, let him be
sive, whether, or
socius, -a, -um, friendly
socius, -i (*m*), ally, friend
sol, solis (*m*), sun
soleo, -ere, solitus sum, to be accustomed
solidus, -a, -um, solid
solium, -i (*n*), throne
sollemnis, -is, -e, solemn, religious

solus, -a, -um, alone
solvo, -ere, solvi, solutum, to set free, dismiss
somnus, -i (*m*), sleep, dream
sonitus, -us (*m*), sound
sono, -are, -ui, -itum, to sound
sonorus, -a, -um, loud-sounding
sonus, -i (*m*), sound
sopio (4), to lull to sleep, deprive of sense
sopor, -oris (*m*), sleep
sors, sortis (*f*), lot, lottery
species, -ei (*f*), sight
speculor (1), to watch
sperno, -ere, sprevi, spretum, to despise
spretus, -a, -um, despised
spes, spei (*f*), hope, prospects
spira, -ae (*f*), coil
splendidus, -a, -um, splendid
spolium, -i (*n*), spoil
spuma, -ae (*f*), foam
spumeus, -a, -um, foaming
spumo (1), to foam
squaleo (2), to be rough or ragged
squameus, -a, -um, scaly
stabulum, -i (*n*), stall, stable
statio, -onis (*f*), anchorage
statuo, -ere, -ui, -utum, to set up, erect, place, construct
stella, -ae (*f*), star
sterno, -ere, stravi, stratum, to lay low, devastate, level, spread
Sthenelus, -i (*m*), Sthenelus (charioteer of Diomede)
stipo (1), to crowd together
sto, stare, steti, statum, to stand
strepitus, -us (*m*), din
strideo, -ere, -di, to creak
stridor, -oris (*m*), creaking
stringo, -ere, -nxi, strictum, to draw (a sword)
studium, -i (*n*), eagerness
stupeo (2), to be amazed, marvel at, stand aghast
stuppeus, -a, -um, made of flax or tow
sub (+ *abl.*), under, beneath
sub (+ *acc.*), towards, up to, close up to
subduco, -ere, -duxi, -ductum, to beach (a ship)
subeo, -ire, -ii, -itum, to come up to, approach, go under, to come to support, to follow
subicio, -ere, -ieci, -iectum, to place under, put under

subito, suddenly
subitus, -a, -um, sudden
sublabor, -i, -lapsus sum, to slip away, glide down
sublatus, -a, -um, *see* **tollo**
submergeo, -ere, -mersi, -mersum, to sink
subnixus, -a, -um, supported, propped up
subsisto, -ere, -stiti, to halt, stop
subvolvo, -ere, to roll up
succedo, -ere, -cessi, -cessum (+ *dat.*), to go under, enter, move towards
successus, -us (*m*), success
succipio, -ere, -cepi, -ceptum, to catch
succurro, -ere, -curri, -cursum (+ *dat.*), to help, occur (to the mind)
suffero, -ferre, sustuli, sublatum, to withstand
sulcus, -i (*m*), furrow
summus, -a, -um, highest, upper, top of, top(most), last
sumo, -ere, sumpsi, sumptum, to take up (arms)
super, besides, on top
  satis superque enough and more than enough
super (+ *acc.*), (fall) on top of
super (+ *abl.*), concerning, on
superbus, -a, -um, proud
superemineo, -ere, to rise above
superi, -orum (*m.pl*), the gods above
supero (1), to tower above, rise above, survive
superus, -a, -um, on high, above
supplex, -icis (*m*), suppliant
surgo, -ere, surrexi, surrectum, to rise
sus, suis (*m/f*), pig
suspectus, -a, -um, suspected
suspensus, -a, -um, anxious
suspicio, -ere, -spexi, -spectum, to look up at
suus, -a, -um, his, her, its, their
Sychaeus, -i (*m*), Sychaeus (Dido's husband)
syrtis, -is (*f*), sandbank

T

tabens, -entis, dripping
tabula, -ae (*f*), plank
tacitus, -a, -um, silent
talis, -is, -e, such
  talia, as follows
tam, so
tamen, however
tandem, at last, (impatiently) for it is high time

tango, -ere, tetigi, tactum, to touch
tantum, only, so much
tantus, -a, -um, so great
taurus, -i (*m*), bull
tectum, -i (*n*), roof, tile, building, house
tego, -ere, texi, tectum, to conceal, protect
tellus, -uris (*f*), land
telum, -i (*n*), weapon
tempero (1), to control
tempestas, -atis (*f*), storm
templum, -i (*n*), temple
tempto (1), to attempt, explore
tempus, -oris (*n*), time, situation
   tempora, -um (*n.pl*), temples (of head)
tendo, -ere, tetendi, tensum, to stretch, strain, struggle, travel, make one's way, pitch a tent
Tenedos, -i (*f*), Tenedos (island off the coast of Troas)
teneo, -ere, -ui, tentum, to hold, inhabit, reach
tener, -era, -erum, tender
tenuis, -is, -e, thin
tenus (+ *abl.*), as far as
ter, three times
terebro (1), to bore through
tergum, -i (*n*), back
tergus, tergoris (*n*), back, hide
terra, -ae (*f*), land
terreo (2), to terrify
testudo, -inis (*f*), dome, penthouse of shields
Teucri, -orum (*m.pl*), Trojans
Teucria, -ae (*f*), Troy
texo, -ere, -ui, textum, to weave
thalamus, -i (*m*), marriage-chamber
theatrum, -i (*n*), theatre
Thessandrus, -i (*m*), Thessandrus (a Greek)
Thybris, -is (*m*), Tiber
Thymoetes, -is (*m*), Thymoetes (a Trojan)
thymum, -i (*n*), thyme
timeo (2), to fear
timor, -oris (*m*), fear
tollo, -ere, sustuli, sublatum, to raise, lift, remove
tondeo, -ere, totondi, tonsum, to clip, cut
torqueo, -ere, torsi, tortum, to drive, hurl
torrens, -entis (*m*), torrent
torreo, -ere, -ui, tostum, to roast, bake

torus, -i (*m*), couch
tot, so many
totus, -a, -um, all, whole
traho, -ere, traxi, tractum, to drag, draw
tranquillus, -a, -um, calm
tremefactus, -a, -um, trembling
tremo, -ere, -ui, to tremble
trepido (1), to tremble, hasten (in fear)
trepidus, -a, -um, fearful, alarmed
tres, tres, tria, three
tristis, -is, -e, sad, stern, shocking, cruel, deplorable
tridens, -entis (*m*), trident
Tritonia, -ae (*f*), Pallas Athene
Tritonis, -idos (*f*), Pallas Athene
Troes, -um (*m.pl*), Trojans
Troia, -ae (*f*), Troy
Troianus, -a, -um, Trojan
Troius, -a, -um, Trojan
Tros, Trois (*m*), a Trojan
trucido (1), to butcher, massacre
tu, you
tuba, -ae (*f*), trumpet
tueor, -eri, tuitus sum, to gaze at, protect
tuli, *see* **fero**
tum, then
tumeo (2), to swell, puff out
tumidus, -a, -um, swelling
tumultus, -us (*m*), uproar, disorder
tumulus, -i (*m*), mound, small hill
tunc, then, at that time
turba, -ae (*f*), crowd
turbo (1), to disturb, throw into confusion
turbo, -inis (*m*), blast, whirlwind
turpis, -is, -e, dishonourable
turris, -is (*f*), tower
tutor (1), to protect
tutus, -a, -um, safe
tuus, -a, -um, your
tui, -orum (*m.pl*), your people
Tydides, -ae (*m*), Diomede (son of Tydeus)
Tyrius, -i (*m*), Tyrian, from Tyre (town in Phoenicia)
Tyrrhenus, -a, -um, Tyrrhenian, Tuscan

U

uber, uberis (*n*), richness
ubi, when, where
ubique, everywhere
Ulixes, -is or **-i,** Ulysses (Greek warrior; also called Odysseus)
ullus, -a, -um, any

ultimus, -a, -um, last
ultro, first, freely, unasked, of one's own accord
ululo (1), to howl
umbo, -onis (*m*), boss (of shield)
umbra, -ae (*f*), shadow
umerus, -i (*m*), shoulder
umquam, ever
una, together
unda, -ae (*f*), wave
unde, whence, from which
undique, from all sides
unus, -a, -um, one, alone, (with superlative) the -est of all men
urbs, urbis (*f*), city
urgeo, -ere, ursi, to drive, press upon
uro, -ere, ussi, ustum, to burn
usquam, anywhere
ut or uti (+ *indic.*), when, how
  ut primum, as soon as
ut (+ *subj.*), so that
uterque, utraque, utrumque, each
uterus, -i (*m*), belly
utinam, would that, I wish that
utor, -i, usus sum (+ *abl.*), to use

V

vacuus, -a, -um, empty
vado, -ere, to advance
vale! farewell!
valeo (2), to be strong, be able
validus, -a, -um, strong, sturdy, mighty
vallis, -is (*f*), valley
vanus, -a, -um, empty, idle (question)
varius, -a, -um, varying, changing, varied
vasto (1), to lay waste, destroy
vastus, -a, -um, huge
-ve, or
veho, -ere, vexi, vectum, to carry
velamen, -inis (*n*), cloak
velim, I would like
vello, -ere, vulsi, vulsum, to tear away
velo (1), to cover, wrap
velum, -i (*n*), sail
velut, as, just as
venenum, -i (*n*), poison
venio, -ire, veni, ventum, to come
ventus, -i (*m*), wind
Venus, Veneris (*f*), Venus (goddess of love, mother of Aeneas)
verbum, -i (*n*), word
vero, truly, in truth
verro, -ere, verri, versum, to sweep, drive along
verso (1), to turn, meditate
vertex, -icis (*m*), head, top

verto, -ere, verti, versum, to turn, overthrow
veru, -us (*n*), spit (for roasting)
verus, -a, -um, true
vester, -tra, -trum, your
vestibulum, -i (*n*), porch, entrance
vestigium, -i (*n*), track, step, footstep
vestis, -is (*f*), robe, clothing
vetus, veteris, old
vetustus, -a, -um, ancient
via, -ae (*f*), street
vibro (1), to quiver
victor, -oris (*m*), conqueror, victorious
victus, -a, -um, vanquished
victus, -us (*m*), food
video, -ere, vidi, visum, to see
  miserabile visu, a pitiful sight to see
videor, -eri, visus sum, to seem
vigil, -ilis (*m*), watchman
viginti, twenty
villus, -i (*m*), nap (of cloth)
vinclum, -i (*n*), chain
vinco, -ere, vici, victum, to conquer
vinculum, -i (*n*), chain
vinum, -i (*n*), wine
violo (1), to violate, outrage, damage
vir, -i (*m*) (*gen.pl* virum), man, husband, hero
vires, -ium (*f.pl*), strength
virgineus, -a, -um, belonging to a virgin
virgo, -inis (*f*), maiden
virtus, -utis (*f*), courage, uprightness
vis, vim, vi, force, power
viscera, -um (*n.pl*), entrails
viso, -ere, -si, to look at
visus, -us (*m*), sight
vita, -ae (*f*), life
vitta, -ae (*f*), fillet, headband
vivo, -ere, vixi, victum, to live
vivus, -a, -um, living, alive, running (water)
vix, scarcely
vociferor (1), to cry aloud
voco (1), to call, summon
volo, velle, volui, to wish
volucer, -cris, -cre, swift
volvo, -ere, volvi, volutum, to roll, ponder
vosmet = vos (you)
vox, vocis (*f*), voice, word
vulgus, -i (*n*), crowd, herd
vulnus, -eris (*n*), wound
vultus, -us (*m*), face, expression, eyes; (*pl.*) features

Z

Zephyrus, -i (*m*), West Wind